Hitting a Moving Target

Hitting a Moving Target

Preaching to the Changing Needs of Your Church

Rick Ezell

kregel
PUBLICATIONS

Grand Rapids, MI 49501

Hitting a Moving Target: Preaching to the Changing Needs of Your Church

Published by Kregel Publications, a division of Kregel, Inc., P.O. Box 2607, Grand Rapids, MI 49501. Kregel Publications provides trusted, biblical publications for Christian growth and service. Your comments and suggestions are valued.

For more information about Kregel Publications, visit our web site at: www.kregel.com

Cover design: Frank Gutbrod
Book design: Nicholas G. Richardson

Library of Congress Cataloging-in-Publication Data
Ezell, Rick.
   Hitting a moving target: preaching to the changing needs of your church / Rick Ezell.
     p.   cm.
   Includes bibliographical references.
   1. Preaching—History. I. Title.
BV4211.2.E96   1999   251—dc21   99-26310
                                        CIP

ISBN 0-8254-2528-x

Printed in the United States of America

1 2 3 4 5 / 03 02 01 00 99

To three very special ladies in my life:

Cindy, my wife
Bailey, my daughter
Grace, my mother

TABLE OF CONTENTS

PREFACE

Are you a Christian public speaker (such as a pastor)? Do you find that the groups whom you address have radically changed in recent years? Do you go from one speaking engagement to the next struggling to make your messages connect with your target audience? Do you long for help in proclaiming God's truth in a way that is life-transforming?

If you answered *yes* to any of these questions, then this book is for you! *Hitting a Moving Target* is not just another dreary text about public speaking. It's a practical and relevant manual on how to reach the people next door, down the street, and in your local community—people just like you—with powerful messages based on Scripture.

I'm convinced that to be effective in our public speaking we must build a bridge between the truth of the Bible and the needs of people. But what are those needs? Some glibly remark that all people have the same sorts of concerns and problems. In a sense this is true. And yet many Christian public speakers fail to connect with their audiences because they have only a vague notion of what their listeners need. These sincere but ineffective communicators have no idea what struggles and successes, joys and pains their listeners have. What's worse, these speakers are clueless about how to change the way they preach and teach.

Do you sometimes find yourself feeling this way? If so, don't despair! In the pages that follow, I will show you how to identify and address the real needs of the people in your audience. Learning how to do this will enable you to be more powerful and life-transforming in your public speaking.

Before you go any further, take a few moments to skim through the chapters of this book. You will discover that *Hitting a Moving Target* will help you to gather, document, and make use of readily available information about your parishioners. You can use this data to better understand and (therefore) to effectively address the issues facing your audience. This book will help you to pinpoint pressing needs quickly and then address them from a biblical text using effective communication tools. I believe that as a busy public speaker, you'll find this manual to be a treasure chest of useful and insightful information.

Unlike men and women of previous generations, the people of today receive much of their information through visual media (television, videos, and computers, to name a few). That's why I've chosen to use a bull's-eye target as the consistent metaphor throughout this book. With this visual symbol forming the backdrop of the discussion, I will show that when you speak in public, you must consider the following: the prevailing culture of your target audience, the local community where your listeners live, the facility where the speaking event takes place, and the people who listen to you speak.

As you study *Hitting a Moving Target,* you will discover realistic, hands-on resources that will make you a powerful messenger for Christ year in and year out. You will find suggestions on how to become an expert not only at presenting God's Word but also at understanding your target audience. In Bible college and seminary you may have learned how to exegete Scripture. In this book you will develop the ability to exegete your community and target audience. Just imagine the transformation that will take place in your public speaking!

My passion for writing comes from Christian public speaking in a setting where the target audience changes about every three years. You might initially think that with such a high turnover rate, it would be nearly impossible to experience any measurable church growth. Not so! Despite the constant change, my church has grown steadily throughout my tenure.

How is that possible? My listeners repeatedly tell me that my sermons meet their needs, so I believe one reason for the sustained growth is the messages I deliver. People seem to appreciate the fact that my messages address life issues from a biblical perspective. It's not surprising, then, that they consider Naperville Baptist their church home. (Of course, God's grace has enabled me consistently to hit the ever-changing target audience through much prayer, study, and reflection.)

My prayer is that this book will prove to be a useful resource to you. And my hope is that you will wear out *Hitting a Moving Target* as you refer to it time and again for help in effectively addressing the needs of your target audience. Remember, the eternal destiny of countless souls could be at stake!

RICK EZELL, D.MIN.
Senior Pastor
Naperville Baptist Church
Naperville, Illinois

CHAPTER ONE

READY, AIM, FIRE?

The greatest obstacle to communication is the
illusion that it has been achieved.
—Marshall McLuhan

I once read a funny story about a little boy who was doing some target shooting one day with his bow and arrows. He would pull the string back as far as he could and then let the arrow fly into the fence. Then he would run over to the fence with a piece of chalk and draw a target around the arrow.

A little girl showed up, saw what he was doing, and became hysterical. "That's not the way to practice!" she shouted. "You're supposed to draw the target and then shoot at it!" But the unrepentant boy dismissed her criticism by saying, "If you do it my way, you never miss!"

Unfortunately this same logic has been behind a lot of my public speaking. I would fire messages at my target audience each week. And if the messages happened to hit anyone's needs, I'd think, "That was my target all along!" While I engaged in biblical exegesis (by using all of my interpretative skills to better understand the sacred text), and while I spoke persuasively (by using all of my oratory skills to communicate with the audience), I had a dismal knowledge and understanding of my listeners.

Someone once said that if you aim at nothing, you'll hit it every time. Sadly, I was speaking from the pulpit and then drawing a

target around whatever needs I happened to "hit." It didn't matter
whether I addressed the concerns of my target audience, for I
was settling for puny results. I was embarrassed to admit that
this was the incredibly calloused approach I took to the all-
important task of communicating God's message of comfort and
cheer to hurting people. Many were coming to my church for
answers, assistance, and aid, and all I could do was fire public
speaking arrows that missed the target.

Underlying effective homiletics is the presentation of the timeless truths of Scripture so that answers to people's questions are
presented, their problems are overcome, and they receive hope
in the midst of their hurts. In order for public speaking in a contemporary context to be a life-transforming event, we must address the specific needs of our audience. It's true that some needs
and issues are apparent in all people in all contexts. Yet we often overlook the particular needs of a specific group of people.
This fact especially rings true in a growing church setting, and
even more so in a highly transitional setting. Identifying and
addressing the abundance of needs will enable us to deliver biblical messages more effectively and powerfully, regardless of
whether our proclamation of God's truth is expository, topical,
or verse-by-verse.

As Christian public speakers, we are challenged by the fact
that the "target" (namely, our audience and their specific needs)
keeps moving. No longer do we address the same people week
in and week out, much less year in and year out. Audiences are
forever changing. Consider the minister of a congregation.
Whereas in the past it seemed that the pastor moved every two
to four years, now it is the members of the church who are moving every two to four years.

The following chapters will give you a step-by-step approach
to gather, document, and utilize readily available information so
that you can better address the issues of an audience in transition. You will learn how to present your messages in such a way
that your listeners consistently get the point you want to make.

In order to visualize the task, picture a target with its concentric circles around a bull's-eye. The center represents the most pressing concerns of your audience. Each successive outer ring symbolizes the various layers of needs they have. The closer rings denote the more urgent issues in their lives. Remember, it's your goal to hit the bull's-eye regularly with your message. You can do this by pinpointing the needs of the people you are speaking to and then addressing those needs from a biblical text using effective communication techniques.

Let's take a few moments to review what's ahead in this book. In chapter 2 you'll discover that we are a mobile society. This is true both locally and nationally, and it is a catalyst for change within our nation. Knowing this will help you to recognize your target audience. In chapter 3 you'll learn how to discern the culture and read the times. This will enable you to make some accurate assumptions about your target audience and thereby get a fix on them. Chapter 4 will give you a strategy for defining your community. You'll discover how to research and identify the make-up and character of your listeners (represented by the outer rings of the bull's-eye). This in turn will help you to bring your target audience into focus.

Chapter 5 will help you to take aim at your listeners by showing you how to identify and assess their particular needs. Chapter 6 discusses how you can appraise the information you obtain about your community and target audience. This will equip you to lock onto them. Chapter 7 describes the profile of the message that will give you maximum impact on your listeners. In other words, you will learn to "fire the right arrow." Chapter 8 discusses how presenting culturally relevant messages enables you to hit the bull's-eye. Finally, in chapter 9 you'll discover how to take stock of your message. You will be shown how to ask and answer the question, "Did the target audience get my point?" Successfully addressing these issues will enable you to score a direct hit every time with amazing accuracy!

CHAPTER TWO

RECOGNIZING THE TARGET AUDIENCE

A sermon at its best is a particular message from a particular person on a particular occasion for a particular audience.
—Raymond Bailey

After accepting the call to my present congregation, I met with church consultant Lyle Schaller, who has resided in the community for years. He told me more about the city and its people in an hour than all the demographic studies I had read for the past few months. But here's the comment that raised my eyebrows: "Be careful what you ask your people to vote for. In this town, they'll vote in favor of anything—in the city, a new tax increase; in the church, a new building program—even when it's not needed." "Why is that?" I inquired. "Because they know they will not be around to pay for it. They'll be gone. Transferred," he responded.

Several years later our church voted to build a needed two-million-dollar sanctuary and educational facility. In a building committee meeting one night we were bellyaching about the budget receipts not keeping pace with our financial projections and the significant number of families that had come and gone. One member of the building committee disclosed that his wife had found an old church directory and crossed off the families that were no longer involved in our congregation. He shared the results by saying, "We have lost fifty-six families in two and a half years."

Schaller's words seemed almost prophetic: "They'll vote for anything because they won't be around to pay for it." Sure, new families had joined our church during this time, but that did not ease the painful pit in my stomach as I drove home that night.

The mobility of Americans is nothing new. Since the days of the wagon trains, we Americans have been on the go from place to place. The rate of mobility increased significantly after World War II, due to the returning servicemen and women, who were now used to relocating often, and also due to the rapid expansion of the peacetime economy. With the increased urbanization and economic upheaval presently at work in our country, there is every reason to expect that increased mobility will continue. Yes, this is not a new phenomenon. But the last few generations of Americans have refined and perfected their ability to be mobile.

We truly are a nation on the move. The Carole King song rings true for our society: "Doesn't anybody stay in one place anymore?"[1] America is the land of the upwardly mobile. Often the emphasis has been placed on *upwardly*. But now it is time to take a closer look at the word *mobile*.

According to the United States Census Bureau, 16 million American households containing 43 million people moved between March 1991 and March 1992.[2] This rate has been consistent for the last several years. This means that one in five people, or 20 percent of the population, change their place of residence each year. Think about it this way—every ten years between 40 and 60 percent of an average American town's population leaves. When all the moves are combined in a lifetime, the average American will uproot about fourteen times.

Some are first-time movers; they're leaving the parental nest for college, marriage, or their own apartment. Others are last-time movers; they're retiring to warmer climates. Many don't move very far, perhaps just across town to a bigger and better house. Others go halfway across the continent in search of a better life.

Among the uprooted, one group is clearly identifiable. These are the families who move, not because they have to and not because they necessarily want to, but because the breadwinner of the family is being transferred (or "relocated") by "the company." Paula Mergenhagen in *Targeting Transitions* reports that 5.4 million households made long-distance moves in 1991–92.[3]

Among these people are the corporate uprooted, and their tribe is increasing constantly. They tend to be repeaters, too. Also among this group, two out of every five households move every three years, and one out of five actually move annually.[4] In today's large national (if not international) companies, the typical transferee is a part of middle management. The move may mean a promotion, or it may be a lateral transfer for the convenience of the company. Or it may be a group move in which an entire division is relocated. It is less regarded as an honor and more often as a duty. And in many cases the transferee will not only be asked to move again, but again and again.

There are other moves that must not be overlooked. A generation ago it was common for couples to marry in their early twenties and stay married for a lifetime. Now people are marrying later, and the divorce rate is getting ever higher. Also, the birth of children presents its share of stresses and changes. The care of aging parents and relatives by middle-age people is a new transition that often requires one or both parties to move. Graduation from institutions of higher learning presents a different set of needs and moves. People in the work place are changing careers and jobs— some of these are self-imposed, while others are the result of corporate restructuring—that often necessitate a move. People are now retiring earlier and living longer in different residences.

While mobility is mostly a matter of physical relocation, it is also an intellectual and emotional issue. Today, one does not need to change addresses in order to be mobile. A person can keep the same address and change jobs, churches, marriages, families, and children.

MOVING DENTS AND DINGS

When people are in transition, not only does the move scratch and abuse the furniture, it also dents and dings the psyche. Susan Miller states in her book, *After the Boxes are Unpacked,* that moving is one of the top ten traumas of life.[5] Geographic moves are life's fourth most stressful event, behind the death of a spouse, divorce, and retirement.[6] Audrey McCollum writes in *The Trauma of Moving,* "Leaving behind a broken rocking chair in which the firstborn was soothed to sleep, a piano around which there was caroling at Christmas, a rusty tricycle—whatever embodies special memories and experiences—can feel like an amputation. It is the loss of a segment of family continuity, of personal history, the loss of a fragment of self."[7]

In the transition of a move, people experience the feeling of detachment from someone or something. The pain of separation and the sense of rootlessness often leave people feeling wounded, which adversely affects their ability to start over. Children are not immune to the pain associated with transitions, either. A *Parents* magazine article states that "toddlers will mourn the loss of their room and of the house they've always lived in. School-age children will mourn the loss of their friends and the loss of their school. Teenagers, along with mourning all of the above, are likely to feel anger at their parents for a major change that is beyond their control."[8] Everyone in the family is potentially scarred and damaged by the move.

Ted and Nancy moved to our community from Texas. They both have master's degrees and are on an upward track in their management jobs with large corporations. They work hard and long, which gives them little time for outside pursuits. What little time they have is spent with their family of two elementary age sons. While they make a lot of money, they also spend a lot of money (especially on their home), and they choose to put much of their purchases on credit cards. They came to me recently teetering on burnout and wondering whether the price they paid for success was too steep.

Ted and Nancy are not alone. Bill, a corporate executive,

recently spoke to me following a message I had given on the purpose of life. He said, "I hate that kind of message." I wondered why. Bill seems to have all of life together: an excellent job with a major oil company, a beautiful family, and all the toys and gadgets normally associated with a successful life. But a message on the meaning of life brought him under conviction. He has relocated a half-dozen times in his short adult life, simply because the job demanded it. While those moves have increased his net-worth, he questions his self-worth.

Sally, a single adult computer programmer, moved to our city six months ago. She has been torn away from family and friends and transplanted to a new place where she does not know any-one. She hungers for community and social contact. She called recently to ask whether I knew anyone her age with similar in-terests that she could hook up with.

As I have watched these upwardly mobile people arrive and leave, I have come to realize that the church is in a tremendous position to provide a stable and healthy environment for relational and spiritual growth. People during times of transition have needs that become heightened and more glaring, such as marital prob-lems, financial concerns, and parenting issues. My church and I have an open window for assisting such people. Life's transitions are the most teachable moments. Granted, determining those needs sometimes can be a challenge. But once they are determined and addressed, the church is well on its way to being a life-giving spring of support, encouragement, and help to hurting people.

THE REVOLVING DOOR

Naperville, Illinois (where I live), is a virtual revolving door to people moving in and then moving out, especially with re-spect to the corporate moves. The city has had an outstanding growth rate in the past twenty-five years. Naperville's 1998 popu-lation was 120,000,[9] giving it the rank of third-largest city in Il-linois. But in 1980 it was the twenty-ninth largest city in the state.[10] Much of its recent growth is due to the relocation of middle- and upper-management personnel.

The revolving door syndrome is also present in the church. People seem to go out the back door as fast as they're coming in the front door. The following scene has been repeated more times than I care to remember during my tenure at Naperville Baptist Church. My secretary buzzed me that I had a call from an active lay leader in the church. Suddenly my heart rate increased, my hands became clammy, and my stomach churned. I had heard through the grapevine that he and his family might be moving. *Oh, no,* I thought, *please don't let it be another one.*

"Hello, Jim," I answered, trying to be cheerful and upbeat. "Hi, Rick. Got a few minutes?" Jim asked. "Sure. What's up?" "Rick, I don't know how to tell you this. I know a lot of people in the church have been transferred recently. I know how difficult that is on the church and on you. But Rick, I'm sorry to have to tell you this. My company has offered me a big promotion that requires that we move out of state. I can't turn it down. Rick, I'm sorry, but we'll be gone as soon as our house sells." I hung up the phone and wept.

I've learned over the years that the same folks who move into the city also move out. The Naperville Chamber of Commerce estimates that the average newcomer will stay little more than three years. Many of its immigrants are middle managers at large corporations who are transferred frequently, or they are highly specialized technocrats who switch jobs often.[11] Several families who have walked through the door of Naperville Baptist Church, only to leave soon for another city, have returned to the congregation again. One church family has called Naperville their home on three separate occasions.

As one can imagine this intense mobility impacts the stability of schools, churches, athletic teams, and civic clubs. Of the 138 suburbs in the Chicago metropolitan area, Naperville ranks 133 in community stability.[12] This mobility has also affected the solidity of Naperville Baptist Church. I was warned about the transitional nature of this community before I became pastor in June of 1988. In the first year of my ministry, one half of the pastoral search committee that brought me to this church had moved away. The full impact of the transitional nature of the church did not hit home until one day in 1992, when I was looking over a list of the fifty-seven people who had joined Naperville Baptist Church in the first six months of my tenure (July through December of 1988). As I scanned those names, I realized that all but four of those individuals had moved away from our community, and two of the four were my wife and me.

The church office prints congregational directories quarterly just to keep up with the flow of incoming and outgoing people. In addition to this, two pictorial directories have been printed in the last five years. These directories are somewhat of a joke. It takes three to five months from picture taking to delivery of the finished product. The directory is virtually obsolete by the time it arrives because of members who have moved away and the newcomers who have moved in.

While Naperville Baptist Church has been in existence for almost thirty years, it is basically a new church. Like our skin that renews itself every seven years, so too the membership of this church has "renewed" itself on a recurring basis. Due to the constant turnover of people, I feel as if I have pastored four different congregations in the past ten years, each of which has assembled in the same church building and been called by the same name. While our morning worship attendance has more than quadrupled and our Bible Study program has tripled, due to the outflow of members, the church often feels as if it is taking three steps forward and two steps back.

This constant fluctuation in congregational membership not only affects church programs as a whole, but it also deeply concerns long-time members. While I was talking to a resident one day about the mobility rate in our church, she said, "I've lived here for fifteen years. I have seen neighbors come and go. It seems that just when I cultivate a relationship, they move. I can't take it anymore. To decrease the pain of saying 'good-bye,' I no longer say 'hello.'" Such an attitude has deep ramifications on an individual's psyche, as well as inappropriate consequences to the friendliness and acceptance of a congregation toward newcomers.

THE ISSUE

Despite the concerns and feelings I noted above, these new-comers cannot be ignored. If Naperville Baptist Church (or your church) disregards the non-member new residents of its community, it will dry up and die. The heart and life of my congregation are the newcomers. They are wanted and welcomed here!

Newcomers bring their own set of issues, concerns, and needs to the table when they arrive in a different community and in a different church. If you transplant your swedish ivy, trauma is predictable. The leaves will lose their luster, the plant may wither, and it may even die. Similarly, transplanting the human organism also takes its toll. In addition to the inconvenience and the downright hard labor involved in a move, the shock of relocation can result in a multitude of feelings and a plethora of needs.

While the logistical concerns of any family moving into a new community are present, the emotional needs tend to be much greater. Uprooted people have been torn away from family and friends and transplanted to a new place where quite often they do not know anyone. Inbred in such moves is a deep need for community. The person in a new locale has to enter unfamiliar social circles in an attempt to make new friends and build new supportive relationships. Sometimes this is difficult, especially when many established residents are like the parishioner who said, "I don't have any space for any new people in my life. I'm like a 'Lego'® piece with all my holes filled with existing relationships."

The church must address both the newcomer's glaring needs and the needs of those who have been present in the community a long time. A pastor and his congregation have a tremendous opportunity for ministry in assisting these two groups of people in the transitions of life. But determining the specific needs of a particular congregation at a definite time can be a challenge. And if a pastor and his church do not address those needs, the consequences can be detrimental. As Herb Miller noted, "Worship leaders unaware or uncaring about needs indigenous to their particular culture reap the reward of empty pews."[13]

Many people will drive past half a dozen churches and even into the next town, especially if that is where they feel comfortable and where their needs are met.[14] This underscores how important it is to capture the attention of people who are experiencing major transitions in life. Addressing their relevant needs through public speaking is one of the best ways to capture their attention.

THE PRESUPPOSITIONS

From what has been said up to this point, the issue before us as public speakers should be crystal clear. Our world is ever changing, and we, as communicators of God's truth, must be aware of and speak to those changes, especially if we are to be effective in what we say from a podium. People experience certain emotions and reactions due to change. Part of our task is to help them understand why they are experiencing these emotions, and then to offer them hope and help to overcome their hurts. The heart of the matter falls into four areas.

The Church Is Dynamic

Congregations are ever changing. "The church is a chameleon," observes James Gustafson, as he points to the congregation's capacity to adapt to new surroundings and to find colors that fit into various environments.[15] Since a church is in a constant state of flux and adaptation, "an institution for its own survival must come to terms with a changing context."[16] Granted, every congregation in every context is undergoing change. But churches in a *transitional* context undergo change at a heightened rate.

When I was a boy, I used a rope to tie an old tire to a tree branch that was four or five feet off the ground. I then would toss a football through the opening of the tire. After a while I became rather proficient at throwing the ball through the opening in the tire. Then, in order to make the exercise more difficult, I would swing the tire back and forth in an attempt to throw the ball through the opening of the moving target. In time I was able to accomplish this task with a relatively high degree of accuracy.

In high school, I played quarterback on the football team. Now I was passing a football to moving receivers who were being covered by speedy defensive backs. At the same time I was being rushed by large defensive linemen and blitzing linebackers. Suddenly the feat of throwing the ball with accuracy became much more difficult for me. The same mechanics that I used to throw the ball through the tire in my backyard did not fundamentally change when I quarterbacked in high school. However, once I was on the playing field, the need for precision intensified. The pursuit of the rushers and the speed of the receivers made it harder for me to complete a pass.

An analogy can be made to churches. Meeting the needs of the audience in a stable environment is like throwing a football at a moving tire on the tree. Similarly, knowing and understanding the needs of the listeners in a changing environment is like trying to pass the football to a receiver while huge linemen and linebackers are surging toward you. The task can be accomplished, but it is much more difficult.

Church Attenders Are Consumers

In our hurried world, people are looking for benefits, regardless of whether they are mobile. Even in the spiritual arena, people are comparison shoppers. They have little time or desire to engage in those activities that are not meeting their needs. Denominational loyalty and affiliation are in a sharp decline. Denominations are not disappearing, but denominationalism has virtually disappeared. Foremost on the consumer's mind are issues of quality, creativity, and relevance. If a congregation does not scratch where people itch, often they will (and do) go to the church that does.

Christian public speaking (such as preaching and teaching) plays a huge role in attracting these people to church. "Unchurched people today are the ultimate consumers," writes Bill Hybels, the pastor of Willow Creek Community Church, which is located outside of Chicago. "We may not like it, but for every sermon we preach, they're asking, 'Am I interested in that subject or not?'"[17] Messages need to be relevant to daily life. They must be user-friendly and useful on Monday morning. The Christian public speaker wins the loyalty of consumers by practically addressing their relevant needs.

Public Speaking Requires Preparation

The preparation for a Sunday message and worship is often like preparing for a Thanksgiving meal, but with one huge difference. The public speaking task is done at least once a week. In contrast, Thanksgiving occurs only once a year (unfortunately!). Hours of thought, coordination, and effort go into this event, which lasts only a short time.

The public speaking task requires a preparation that recognizes the importance of knowing the text to be presented and coordinating the worship with the message. Sadly, an equally important factor that is often ignored concerns the character and needs of the audience being addressed. Speakers often make gargantuan (and frequently incorrect) assumptions about their listeners. Clyde Fant, writing in *Preaching for Today*, noted, "Our sermons cannot reflect profound knowledge of the first century and abysmal ignorance of the twentieth century. No one can be true to the biblical text and ignore the congregation. The biblical word is never a word in abstraction. It is always a specific word to a specific situation."[18]

Christian public speakers must listen to God's Word personally. But they must also be attuned to how Scripture can meet the specific needs of a particular group being addressed. Thus, preparation for public speaking is a commitment to listen to the text as well as to the needs of the target audience. When the living Word touches the living situation, the speaker makes a real and life-transforming connection with the hearers.

Reginald Fuller maintained that the task of the Christian public speaker is to build a bridge between the poles of the text and the contemporary situation. In order for the building of this bridge to occur, the spokesperson needs to know as much as possible about both poles. Fuller wrote, "Not only do they need to know the Bible, but also they need to know all they can about the contemporary world and its culture."[19]

Fred Craddock referred to this process as the two focal points of study. He wrote, "One focus is upon the listeners, including their contexts: personal, domestic, social, political, economic. The other is upon the biblical text, including its contexts: historical, theological, and literary. . . . What the listeners hear the text say in a fresh, appropriate, and indigenous way to them: that is the message for the sermon."[20] From this we see that the Christian public speaker must know and understand the target audience in order to speak to their hurts and concerns. Only when communicators of God's truth erect the bridge between themselves and their listeners will their efforts to communicate effectively be successful.

Knowledge Is Invaluable

The adage often heard today is that "knowledge is power." It also has been said that we are living in the "Age of Information." These two statements may well be true. As our country has gone from having a manufacturing-based economy to having a service-based economy, the availability of information has become essential to its ongoing prosperity. And with that information comes power. George Barna says, "Those who possess and utilize information most effectively are those who stand the greatest chance of succeeding in the marketplace."[21]

A similar argument could be made for Christian public speaking. Knowing and understanding one's hearers "enables the minister to preach with a power and effectiveness."[22] Fred Craddock says that "the most effective preachers in this or any generation are pastors, whose names we may or may not ever know, but they recognize . . . the central importance of knowing one's hearers, a fact which makes it possible for the sermon to have that irreplaceable source of power: appropriateness. Many otherwise good sermons make no contact because they are to the wrong people at the wrong time."[23]

These presuppositions lead to the following basic question:

"Can Christian public speaking address the needs of people in a mobile, ever-changing society?" The answer is *yes,* especially if the speaker can identify and address the pressing needs of the target audience. Of course, that's a big *if*. In order for that condition to be satisfied, the speaker must clearly and accurately identify his or her listeners.

Peter Marshall, the famous Presbyterian minister and chaplain of the Senate, used to say, "We preachers often answer questions no one is asking." Tragically, in today's context, we Christian public speakers often address people that we don't know. In order for us to be effective in what we say from the podium, we need to establish a common ground with our target audience. Incidentally, the word *communication* comes from the Latin term *communis,* which means "common." As Howard Hendricks has pointed out, "the greater the commonality, the greater the potential for communication."[24]

We must know our listeners better than they know themselves. In other words, we must be sensitive to their feelings, hurts, and aspirations. In addition, we must be attuned to what drives and motivates our target audience. We need to consider what spiritual components are missing from their lives that would bring them meaning and fulfillment. Of course, we don't need to know everything, but we are wise to discover the bedrock issues in the lives of our listeners. Calvin Miller, in his book entitled *Marketplace Preaching,* urges Christian public speakers "to get outside the walls and find out once again what people are talking about and what their interests and needs really are."[25] In doing so, the speaker can talk not only their language, but also crawl into their minds and speak to their hurts. And in doing so, the speaker discovers the spiritual "hot buttons" of their lives.

To establish this common ground, the speaker needs to exegete both the biblical text and the community context. This can be done by answering some important questions about the target audience. Who are these people? Where are they? What are they thinking? How are they feeling? What are their needs? What are their hurts? What are their interests? What are their temptations? What is their idolatry? Where is their sin? How are they seeking God? With what spiritual matters are they wrestling? Ultimately, the Christian public speaker needs to ask, "What is the good news they need to hear?

Obtaining this information takes time. In fact, it's more like a process than a one-time event. Despite the sacrifice and effort involved in getting the facts, it's worth it, for the speaker is better able to aim accurately at the target audience. With this common ground forming the backdrop of what is said, the speaker can deliver a relevant, encouraging message on each and every occasion. And once the information has been assessed and classified, it can be used again and again to touch the heart and soul of one's listeners.

So far we have learned how to recognize the target audience. In the next chapter we will discover how to get a fix on them. Yes, the task is formidable. But with God's help we can rise to the challenge!

ENDNOTES

1. Carole King, "So Far Away" (Hollywood: Colgens—ENI Music, 1971).
2. Paula Mergenhagen, *Targeting Transitions* (Ithaca, N.Y.: American Demographics, 1995), 208.
3. Ibid., 207–208.
4. Ronald J. Raymond, Jr. and Stephen V. Eliot, *Grow Your Roots Anywhere, Anytime* (Ridgefield, Conn.: Peter H. Wyden, 1980), 4.
5. Susan Miller, *After the Boxes Are Unpacked* (Colorado Springs: Focus on the Family, 1995), v.
6. Mergenhagen, *Targeting Transitions,* 244.
7. Audrey T. McCollum, *The Trauma of Moving: Psychological Issues for Women* (Newbury Park, Calif.: Sage, 1990), 71.
8. Susan Mernit quoting from Marilyn Segal in "Good-bye House," *Parents Magazine,* May 1990, 117.
9. Naperville Chamber of Commerce.
10. "1990 Census Population Data for Illinois Counties and Incorporated Places" (Illinois Department of Public Health), 12. In 1980, the population of Naperville was 42,330.
11. Stevenson Swanson, "Growing Pains," *The Chicago Tribune,* Sunday, 25 October 1987, 20.

12. 1990 Census for Illinois, 12.
13. Herb Miller, *How to Build a Magnetic Church*, Creative Leadership Series, ed. Lyle E. Schaller (Nashville: Abingdon, 1987), 50.
14. Leith Anderson, *Dying for Change* (Minneapolis: Bethany House, 1990), 35.
15. James Gustafson, *Treasure in Earthen Vessels* (New York: Harper and Bros., 1961), 112.
16. Jackson W. Carroll, Carl S. Dudley, and William McKinney, *Handbook for Congregational Studies* (Nashville: Abingdon, 1986), 48.
17. Bill Hybels, "Speaking to the Secularized Mind," *Mastering Contemporary Preaching* (Portland: Multnomah/Christianity Today, 1989), 31.
18. Clyde E. Fant, *Preaching for Today* (New York: Harper and Row, 1975), 105.
19. Reginald H. Fuller, *The Use of the Bible in Preaching* (Philadelphia: Fortress, 1981), 41.
20. Fred B. Craddock, *Preaching* (Nashville: Abingdon, 1985), 85.
21. George Barna, *Marketing the Church* (Colorado Springs: NavPress, 1988), 62.
22. Craddock, *Preaching*, 91.
23. Ibid., 91–92.
24. Howard Hendricks, *Teaching to Change Lives* (Portland: Multnomah, 1987), 98.
25. Calvin Miller, *Marketplace Preaching* (Grand Rapids: Baker, 1995), 19.

CHAPTER THREE

GETTING A FIX ON THE TARGET AUDIENCE

The gospel is always communicated in the terms
of some culture. The only question is, which one?
—Rick Warren

Each summer for the past several years my family has vacationed in a small Florida town on the Atlantic coast. While we are away from the crowds and the hustle and bustle of the city, the biggest decision we have to make each day is whether to go to the ocean or the pool. It is my kind of vacation! When we walk to the beach, we not only take our towels, sun screen, and umbrella, but also our boogie boards. These are two-feet by three-feet hard plastic boards that we use to ride the waves into the shore.

I have made some rather astute observations during those vacations, especially while I'm resting on a boogie board and waiting in the warm ocean water for the next wave to bring me to the beach.

- Waves are always changing and unpredictable in their movements.
- Never turn your back for long to the waves, especially when you are close to the shore.
- Don't watch in envy people who are catching waves to either

side of you, for you are more likely to miss the "big one" that's coming toward you.

- If you catch a wave too soon, you'll swallow a lot of water.
- If you catch a wave too late, it will surge over you.
- If you catch a wave at just the right time, you'll experience the ride of your life.
- Knowing which waves to let pass and which ones to take is the key to experiencing great rides.
- Knowing how to get off the wave before it hurls you onto the beach will prevent you from getting scraped elbows and knees.

As I study the waves to detect the perfect one to ride, I have to be constantly watching, waiting, and preparing myself for the right moment. Sometimes I have to move slightly to the right or to the left to catch the big wave. But when I do, look out! I know that I'm in for a thrill!

One day while I was resting on my boogie board and anticipating the next wave to come my way, I made this keen observation. Effective Christian public speakers, like effective boogie boarders, must understand the waves of the culture in which they live. One of my responsibilities as a communicator of the gospel is to learn how to read those cultural "waves." It's not my responsibility to make waves, but to recognize the signs of what is happening around me. The more perceptive I am at knowing which waves to pass and which ones to ride will not only make me more stalwart as a church leader, but also more effective as a communicator of God's truth. When I don't read the waves correctly, I may experience a "wipeout" both personally and corporately.

A BUSINESS WIPEOUT

Do you ever wish you had been present at the creation of a doomed business strategy? Travel back fifty years to the mahogany-paneled office of Sewell Avery, then chairman of Montgomery Ward & Co. Avery was responsible for Ward's failure to open a single new store from 1941 to 1957. Instead, the big retailer piled up cash—and then sat on it. Ward's amassed working capital of $607 million, earning him a dubious Wall Street nickname: "the bank with the department store front." So why didn't he join in the nation's postwar expansion by following Americans to the suburbs? It's simple. He held firmly to the belief and vision that a depression had followed every major war since the time of Napoleon. "Who am I to argue with history?" Avery demanded. "Why build $14-a-foot buildings when we soon can do it for $3 a foot?"

On the other side of Chicago, Ward's rival, Sears, Roebuck & Co., had a different idea. In 1946, Sears gambled its future and began a costly expansion into suburbia. Had another depression occurred, Sears would have been financially devastated. Instead, within a decade Sears had doubled its revenues, while Ward's stood still. Sears never looked back, and Ward's never caught up. In fact, Ward's eventually went bankrupt. You might say that it experienced a business wipeout.[1]

How could corporate planning go so wrong? Montgomery Ward's postwar troubles sprang from its firm adherence to a bad idea from a different time and culture. Because Sewell Avery thought a depression would follow World War II, and because he failed to see that middle-America was moving to the suburbs, he misread the cultural waves and consequently his business wiped out.

Reading the waves of culture is assessing the events and occurrences taking place around us in our world and drawing conclusions, or educated guesses, about what will happen in our world tomorrow. As a Christian public speaker, I don't need to know the top ten businesses of the new millennium, or the top ten stocks for next year, or even the fashion trends for the fall lineup. But I had better know about the world my hearers will face tomorrow. If I mistake the breaking of the cultural waves, it may cause some in my audience to wipe out for eternity.

Sewell Avery was not the first corporate executive to wipe out, nor will he be the last. Corporations, businesses, churches, and

Christian public speakers do it all the time. Even the people in Jesus' day misread the cultural waves.

LOOKING FOR A SIGN

"The Pharisees and Sadducees came to Jesus and tested him by asking him to show them a sign from heaven" (Matt. 16:1 NIV). It has been said that necessity makes strange bedfellows. Well, hostility and hatred make for even stranger companions! Putting the Pharisees and the Sadducees together was like mixing oil and water, or like the Democrats and Republicans becoming one party, or like liberal and conservative theologians issuing a joint doctrinal statement.

G. Campbell Morgan calls this pairing of religious leaders "the coalition of criticism." The Pharisees were traditionalists, being theologically and politically conservative. They would have never killed Jesus. They might have tried to argue Him to death, but on their own they would hardly have resorted to violence. In contrast, the Sadducees were the rationalists of their day, being theologically and politically liberal. Incidentally, they were more concerned with politics than with religion. They were wealthy, and they saw Jesus as a threat to their privileged status.

While the Pharisees and Sadducees were avowed opponents of each other, they joined forces against Jesus. They consorted together against someone whom they regarded as their common enemy. In this case, they asked for a sign. The term referred to more than a simple miracle or a mere demonstration of power. It also denoted the wonder by which one may recognize a person and confirm his or her identity. The religious leaders wanted tangible proof that Jesus was the Messiah, whom God had sent to Israel. Sadly, the Pharisees and Sadducees failed to read the "waves" of God's presence in Christ. These indicators were all around them (for instance, in the miracles Jesus performed, in the following He had attracted, and in the authority by which He spoke).

Christ did not mince words in responding to the religious leaders' demands. He declared, "When evening comes, you say, 'It will be fair weather, for the sky is red,' and in the morning, 'To-day it will be stormy, for the sky is red and overcast.' You know how to interpret the appearance of the sky, but you cannot in-terpret the signs of the times. A wicked and adulterous genera-tion looks for a miraculous sign, but none will be given it except the sign of Jonah" (vv. 2–4).

Jesus told the Pharisees and Sadducees that discerning the signs of the time could be done as effectively as reading the signs of the weather in the sky. The Lord's response resembles a fa-miliar saying about predicting the weather: "A red sky at night is the sailor's delight; a red sky in the morning is the sailor's warn-ing." The religious leaders were as adept at interpreting the phe-nomenon in the sky regarding the weather as we are at making sense of the stock market report or the box scores and stand-ings in baseball.

The implication is clear. The Pharisees and Sadducees did not lack evidence of what God was doing in their culture through Christ. Rather, they did not have the insight to detect what was happening around them. Similarly, we have lots of information about the cultural forces at work in our world. By carefully ex-amining the evidence, we can draw valid conclusions about our target audience. It's a solemn responsibility that we dare not take lightly.

THE FIRST STEP

Understanding the waves of culture is an important first step in getting a fix on the target audience. *Culture* refers to the lifestyle and mind-set of the society at large. It has to do with what people are feeling, what interests them, what they value, what pains them, and what they fear. If a group of missionar-ies were going to another country, they would first try to un-derstand the culture of that distant land. In today's secular environment, it is just as important for me, a Christian preacher, to understand the culture from which the congregation gath-ers. I don't have to agree with the culture around me, but I had better understand it.

Consider Jesus. He understood the culture to which He spoke. He walked among the people, spoke their language, observed their habits, knew their interests, sensed their fears, and recognized their hurts. He was keenly aware of current events. He could read the waves because He fathomed the culture.

Likewise, for me to impact my culture, I too must fathom it. I could never have learned to ride a boogie board by standing on the beach. I had to get in the water. Rick Warren writes, "I've noticed that whenever I go fishing the fish don't automatically jump into my boat or throw themselves up onto the shore for me. Their culture (under water) is very different from mine (air). It takes intentional effort on my part to make contact with fish. Somehow I must figure out how to get the bait right in front of their nose in their culture."[2]

An element of the prophet's role exists in my public speaking ministry. In Bible times, prophets made a living by predicting future events. This was their job, their ministry, and their calling. As a Christian public speaker, my job description does not come merely from a personnel policy manual. A major part of my calling is to know and understand the waves of the culture. I can't predict the future, but I can interpret the present and discern its effect on the future. Having done that, it's my responsibility as a proclaimer of God's truth to issue a culturally relevant word of warning, caution, and encouragement. I will fail to do this effectively if I don't study what is going on in my world.

Eugene Petersen wrote, "Without study, without the use of our mind in a disciplined way, we are sitting ducks for the culture."[3] So how do I keep from being a sitting duck in a culture that would like to blast me out of the water? Petersen answers, "It's my job to be suspicious of the culture. I'm not a cultural critic, but to be a pastor, I cannot be seduced by the world. This becomes increasingly difficult in this so-called postmodern time. If you're not sharp, you're on the devil's side without knowing it."[4]

Living in Chicago has given me ample opportunity to watch Michael Jordan play basketball. On the court there are times when the athlete looks lazy, as if he's not doing anything. But then he suddenly moves through three opponents on the other team and slam-dunks the ball before a crowd of cheering fans!

As a pastor, how do I slip through the opposition and make my point? I do it by being lazy—or what appears to be laziness. I sit in my study for half a day and read a book that doesn't have anything to do with my sermon. I may also drive through my community to see what new things are happening. I might talk with people at a restaurant, scan the morning newspaper, or attend the weekly Rotary Club luncheon. As a pastor, I've got a responsibility to be aware of the culture so that I can alert my congregation to its pitfalls and dangers and thus prevent them from being blindsided by ignorance. If I don't do this, nobody will.

Here's a word of encouragement: I don't have to be perfect at reading the signs of the time, just better than the competition. Consider the story of two hikers in the woods. One says, "I smell a bear!" and immediately puts on his jogging shoes. The other one snickers and says, "Jogging shoes! You can't outrun a bear!" The first hiker replies with a smile, "I don't have to outrun the bear—I just have to outrun you."

The point is that I can't hope to spot every trend in society, every sign of the times, and every driving force in culture. But by developing a few habits, I am better able to spot the shifts in society and thus prepare, warn, encourage, and speak to my target audience about these changes. The better informed I am, the fewer unpleasant surprises my listeners will receive. Thus, I prepare my messages in order to equip my audience to better anticipate and respond to what potentially lies ahead for them. I seek to be a responder rather than a reactor to societal changes. And hopefully my listeners will one day rise up and call me blessed!

HOW TO READ THE WAVES

How do I penetrate the culture? How do I read the waves of societal change taking place all around me? How can I determine what impact today's events will have on tomorrow? As Jesus noted to the Pharisees and the Sadducees, it's not as difficult as I might think. Perhaps as I go about discerning the signs of the times, some uninformed and uneducated viewers might conclude that I am being lazy. Of course, this isn't true. In fact, it's hard work that never ends. For instance, reading the cultural waves doesn't mean that I just set aside every Thursday afternoon from 1 to 4 P.M. for this chore. I discern the signs of the times as I go about my everyday business. I need to perform the following functions in order to better understand societal influences.

1. *Look at my world.* Yogi Berra spoke an inadvertent mouthful when he said, "You can observe a lot just by watching." David McKenna in his book, *Mega Truth,* talks about one of the smartest persons he ever knew. Harold Pepinsky, a professor at Ohio State University and a household name in social psychology, appeared at the door of McKenna's faculty office one morning wearing an impish grin and a balloon-sized lapel pin. On the pin were emblazoned the big blue letters, "T.O.C.S." McKenna instantly indulged the plea on his colleague's face by asking, "What does 'T.O.C.S.' mean?" With childlike glee, the renowned Dr. Pepinsky's finger walked his way across the letters, announcing as he went, "Thoughtful Observer of the Contemporary Scene."[5] Like Yogi, he knew that people can observe a lot just by watching the world around them.

People in our society admit all too often that they "should have seen it coming." As a Christian public speaker, I have a responsibility to try to spot what is coming down the road so as to better inform my listening audience. Please don't misunderstand me. I don't have to know what will happen ten years from now, or five, or even one. But I should have a feel for what the people in my listening audience will face tomorrow. I should have a sense of what the parents, the business owners, and the students will encounter as they move about their world. I have to look at life through their eyes. I need to understand the struggles that parents face in rearing children in a highly competitive community. I need to feel what corporate managers face with the restructuring and reengineering of their companies. And I need to put myself in the shoes of ninth graders as they venture off to a seemingly cold and impersonal high school.

2. *Eavesdrop on society around me.* My motto is "first look, then listen." What are people saying? What are they thinking? Where are they going? What appears to be the trends? What are some common elements that I see happening in my world? What are the turning points in society?

I can discover a world of information by overhearing what people are saying. For example, a physician in Tennessee was renowned for buying a parcel of land just before a shopping mall located across the street, and stock in a new bank just as it was taking off. Where did he get his information? Most likely he obtained it from his patients. While rendering care, the physician learned about investment opportunities before they were common knowledge. And he was shrewd enough to separate the good tips from the bad ones.

A secretary became a millionaire by buying stock that her boss had purchased. When her attorney boss would talk about a good deal and a hot buy and how he had purchased a hundred or two hundred shares, she would buy one or two. Eventually, these small investments parlayed into a million dollars. Was she an expert in the stock market? Did she read prospectuses? No. She simply overheard some good investments and had the good sense to invest a portion of her money in those stocks. She was attuned to what was going on around her.

As a Christian public speaker, I have myriad weekly contacts. When I probe beneath the surface of things, I discover what is going on in people's heads. I keep my ears perked at social gatherings to listen to the conversations of others, not in a destructive sense mind you, but to note what struggles, joys, and circumstances people are facing. I love to take trips with a group of guys. While I read a book, I listen to their conversations. I gain insight into what is happening in their lives, both at their places of work and within their families. I attend a service club in the community. Seated around a table over lunch, I hear what is going on in the business arena. Often I become aware of information before it becomes public knowledge. This helps me to prepare my congregation for the future impact of possible changes in society. Frequently, I pick up insightful information about their thoughts and feelings simply by putting up my "antennae" and listening.

3. *Talk to people*. One of the best ways to read the waves of cultural change is to talk to people. I don't need to hire a marketing firm. I just need to get out of the office and see what is going on in the world. In his book entitled *Urban Christian*, Ray Bakke suggests "that pastors should invest one day a week in 'networking' their communities—building personal relationships at all levels."[6] He advocates visiting all the other pastors of the churches in the community, the public and voluntary agencies, and the businesses around the church and beyond. As I have visited these people, I found that it is helpful to ask the following insightful questions:

- What makes people happy in this city?
- What do you feel are the greatest needs in our community?
- What three things could be done *today* that would improve the life of our community *tomorrow*?
- What have you discovered about this community?
- How can I work with you and help you do your job better?

I listen for the hurts, interests, needs, and fears of people in my community. No demographic study or psychographic report can replace actually talking with the people in my community. Statistics are helpful, but they paint only part of the picture.

4. *Read*. An effective public speaker is well-read. Understanding culture is more than merely reading material for Sunday's message. Often, if I am not careful, I find myself reading trivia and clutter. I have learned to read so that I can discover the larger picture. Robert Tucker, in his book entitled *Managing the Future*, suggests nine techniques to get more from my reading so that I can understand the waves of cultural change.

- *Read for surprises*. Look for what's different, incongruous, new, worrisome, or exciting. Professional social forecasters call this scanning and monitoring. They scan to monitor trends.

- *Read broadly.* Tucker suggests that business leaders subscribe to at least a dozen magazines and newspapers, even if they don't read them all as they come in. As a public speaker I need to read widely. Even if I only scan the papers and magazines, I will pick up a wealth of information.
- *Read for different points of view.* I never know where a new idea will come from.
- *Read for the wheat and skip the chaff.* I spend time reading the feature stories and skip the celebrity profiles, crime reports, and the latest scandal.
- *Read up on at least one new subject every week.* I make a point of reading a long, in-depth article on a subject that is new and, quite possibly, one in which I'm not initially interested.
- *Read the local newspapers when traveling.* I have found this to be a great way to get a broader, more diversified perspective on what is taking place around me.
- *Subscribe to newsletters and trend reports.* While many of these can be quite expensive, they do provide information that is invaluable.
- *Read the nonfiction best-sellers.* These can be a window into the world around me.
- *Read the mail.* Or more to the point, scan the mail for information on who's doing what and why.[7]

While I continue to read publications from the Christian bookstore, I also have made it a habit to read publications found only in secular bookstores. For instance, I recently read *The Millionaire Next Door*. It's not that I'm a millionaire, or that I will become one. Instead, I read this book because in my upper-middle-class, white-collar community there are several millionaires and many more who want to become one. This book provided me with an abundance of information about wealthy people. I am now better educated and prepared to deal with those people and speak to their needs.

5. *Assess the present.* Peter Drucker has been recognized as the "father of modern management." A recent *Forbes* cover story called him "the most perceptive observer of the American scene since Alexis de Tocqueville." Leadership Network recently excerpted some of his most important lessons. The one that jumped off the fax for me was, "Know the value of foresight. . . . You can't predict the future, but you must assess the futurity of present events."[8]

John Nasbitt wrote *Megatrends* in the 1980s, selling millions of copies, and *Megatrends 2000* in the 1990s. While we may question Naisbitt's methods of research, the soundness of his premises, and the sweep of his observations, no one can dispute the impact of his books upon the American mind. His basic assumption was that we can best predict the future by understanding the present. Just as we need history to interpret the present, we also need the present to predict the future. Otherwise, we are condemned to repeat the past, be unrealistic in the present, and fantasize about the future.

Just as churches that live in the past and utilize the methodologies of a previous generation will grow stale and ineffective, so too will Christian public speakers who fail to assess the present. For me, assessing the present means seriously seeing what is taking place now in the world. I like to ask: What is happening with the church? The family? The church consumer? The marketplace? The involvement of people? The media? The economy? The political scene?

6. *Know what God is doing.* The Scriptures tell me that there are some things that only God can do. I need to have spiritual eyes to identify those things. I have been so ingrained in a cause-and-effect way of doing things, that sometimes I fail to see when God is working. When the Lord is up to something, I need to know it. I want God to open my spiritual eyes so that I can see Him at work.

The Pharisees and Sadducees, who demanded a sign from Jesus, were no different from me. I, too, long for an insider's tip, a favorable projection about the future. The religious leaders failed to see that the sign was there all along. If they had opened their spiritual eyes, they would have understood that Jesus is the Messiah. They would have recognized that His teachings and miracles confirmed His claim to be the Son of God. This incident involving the Pharisees and Sadducees is a poignant reminder to me that I can be religious and miss God, even when His glorious presence is before me.

God is at work when I see someone trust in Christ for salvation, or ask about spiritual matters, or come to understand biblical truth, or experience conviction of sin, or become convinced of the righteousness of Christ, or become aware of the Lord's judgment on sin. God is at work in the big things and in the little things. I often look for God in the miraculous and miss Him in the mundane. Repeatedly I need to ask the following: What is God up to in my life? In my church? In other churches? In my community? In my nation? In my world? By looking through spiritual eyes, I can see the hand of God at work.

As I read the waves of cultural change—by looking, listening, talking, reading, and assessing—I make assumptions about my target audience. These assumptions are nothing more than hunches, guesses, and hypotheses about what is going on in their lives. These assumptions influence my public speaking. Let's face it. We all make assumptions before we speak publicly and even while we prepare a message. We will be more successful at getting a fix on our target audience by doing our homework in reading the waves of cultural change. Then our assumptions about our listeners will become more valid and better defined. Otherwise, quite frankly, we are shooting into the dark.

A FINAL THOUGHT

Despite all that I've said about studying and understanding our culture, I'm reminded of something I read from William Willimon. He wrote, "The Bible doesn't want to *speak* to the modern world; the Bible wants to *convert* the modern world. . . . The point is not to speak to the culture. The point is to change it. God's appointed means of producing change is called 'church'; and God's typical way of producing church is called 'preaching.'"[9]

As Christian public speakers, we are called to be agents of spiritual change in our society. In this chapter we have talked about getting a fix on the target audience. In the next chapter we will consider how to bring them into focus.

ENDNOTES

1. John McCormick, "You Snooze, You Lose," *Newsweek*, 21 July 1997, 50.
2. Rick Warren, *The Purpose-Driven Church* (Grand Rapids: Zondervan, 1995), 196.
3. Eugene Petersen, "Interview," *Leadership*, spring 1997, 25.
4. Ibid., 25–26.
5. David McKenna, *Mega Truth* (San Bernardino, Calif.: Here's Life, 1994), 21.
6. Ray Bakke, *The Urban Christian* (Downers Grove, Ill.: InterVarsity, 1987), 110–11.
7. Robert B. Tucker, *Managing the Future* (New York: Putnam's, 1991), 111–13.
8. "Net Fax, Leadership Network," Dallas, no. 75, July 7, 1997.
9. William Willimon, "This Culture Is Overrated," *Leadership*, winter 1997, 30–31.

CHAPTER FOUR

BRINGING THE TARGET AUDIENCE INTO FOCUS

*Becoming an effective teacher is simple. You just
prepare and prepare until drops of blood appear on
your forehead.*
—Marlene LeFever

Can you imagine a photographer shooting some pictures without taking time to focus the camera? What deer hunter would stand on the top of a hill and shoot randomly into the valley without knowing the exact whereabouts of the animal? Without a focus on our target audience, our efforts at effective communication are only wishful thinking. I admit that it takes time, energy, and some resources to bring the target audience into clear view, but it's worth every minute and every penny. The more focused we are on our listeners, the more likely it is that we will score a direct hit with our message.

Lee Strobel is the Teaching Pastor of Willow Creek Community Church. He's also the author of *Inside the Mind of Unchurched Harry and Mary*. Strobel writes the following concerning the Christian witness that is essential for public speakers: "Christians can't speak the language of the people they're trying to reach until they know who their target audience is going to be."[1] It stands to reason that one will communicate vastly different to an African-American congregation in an inner-city context than to a predominantly Asian congregation in an affluent suburb, or to a middle-class congregation in a rural farming community. Doug Murren is the former pastor of Eastside Foursquare Church, in Kirkland, Washington. He notes that "clearly defining your target group is not only essential to your philosophy of ministry but also vital in ensuring your effectiveness as a successful pastor in a greatly unchurched culture."[2]

Our target audience comes into focus by defining and identifying the community in which they live. In the business world, this methodology is referred to as "knowing your customer." Church researcher George Barna wrote, "The church is a business. It is involved in the business of ministry. As such, the local church must be run with the same wisdom and savvy that characterizes any for-profit business."[3] The local church's success, then, is dependent on impacting a growing share of its market area.

A profile is needed of the typical resident of the community that the church services. Rick Warren is pastor of Saddleback Valley Community Church in Mission Viejo, California. He researched the area surrounding his church and discovered the make-up of the average resident that his congregation was trying to reach. The result was "Saddleback Sam and Samantha," the typical resident of Orange County, California. At Willow Creek Community Church in South Barrington, Illinois, a similar study was conducted, resulting in the typical resident known as "Unchurched Harry and Mary."

Focusing on one's target to communicate the gospel has not been borrowed from advertising executives or marketing analysts. It is as old as the Bible. Jesus repeatedly brought His target audience into focus. For instance, when a Canaanite woman appealed to Him to heal her daughter, Jesus declared that the Father had sent Him to focus on "the lost sheep of Israel" (Matt. 15:24 NIV). Of course, Jesus healed the woman's daughter due to her faith. Yet in this encounter He publicly identified His ministry target as the Jews. Christ initially directed His ministry to a specific group of people in order to be effective, not exclusive.

Each of the gospels was written with a specific target audience in mind. Matthew's gospel was targeted for the Jewish reader; Mark's was intended for the Christians in Rome; Luke wrote to a Gentile audience; and John targeted non-Christian readers. They all had the same essential message, but they wrote with a different audience in mind. Similarly, Paul targeted his ministry to the Gentiles, while Peter focused his attention on the Jews.

Having a clearly defined target is both biblical and effective. And pinpointing precisely the target audience enables the Christian public speaker and the church to focus the teaching and preaching, the programs, and the strategies in a way that most effectively communicates to the needs of the community. When the people in the neighborhood have been researched thoroughly, then the profile of the typical resident begins to take shape.

The adage "information reduces anxiety" applies not only to organizational relationships but also to Christian public speaking. When the preaching and teaching are based on recent and accurate information about the hearers, then the message will connect with the audience, even one that is a moving target. Adequate information about the community's residents reduces the anxiety about speaking to the needs of people. Believers who are serious about making an impact with their public speaking will become experts on their community. They will seek to know more about their neighborhoods than anyone else. As we will see, studying a particular community usually entails several areas of investigation.

GEOGRAPHIC LOCATION

The first concern is the physical whereabouts of the community. Where is your church located and what does that say about your community? Is the area rural, suburban, or urban? What makes this location unique? What are its distinguishing features? What are two or three important characteristics about your community? Obtaining these facts will help you to size up your ministry area and the people that live within it. Once you have obtained this information, write a brief narrative description of your church's geographical location. Do this as though you were preparing an ad slick for your chamber of commerce or a community informational brochure.

The following is the way I would take the facts about the geographical location of my community and put them in a narrative form.

> Naperville, Illinois, is a far western suburb of Chicago. The city is located approximately thirty miles from downtown Chicago, and its proximity makes for easy access to major interstate highways, airports, and passenger and freight railroad systems.
>
> Naperville has become one of the fastest growing communities in the Midwest. The city's ambiance as a master-planned community creates a distinct image that incorporates economic prosperity, outstanding educational opportunities, and high-caliber cultural events. Expanding and diverse high-technology, research, and commercial bases all complement Naperville's continuing growth.
>
> In 1966, AT&T located a branch of Bell Laboratories in Naperville, and this began a period of growth that continues today. The Amoco Research Center came to Naperville in 1969. Additionally, Nalco Chemical Company's worldwide headquarters and Allied Van Lines' worldwide center of operations located in Naperville. These changes brought thousands of new jobs into the area. Northern Illinois Gas, General Motors Corporation, Nabisco Food Company, and the Wall Street Journal's printing plant for the Midwest all make their homes in Naperville.
>
> Two school districts serve the Naperville area. Their academic reputation is confirmed by national student assessment and achievement scores, which are above average in all subjects. The school systems, along with the strong commitment by local leadership to provide a

positive emphasis on families—combined with the other amenities of medical care, climate, shopping, and a low crime rate make Naperville the number one city in America for raising a family.

DEMOGRAPHICS

It is vitally important to gather information about the demographics of the target audience. Demographics are the "hard" facts about a population. They are concerned with the age, income, race, marital status, occupation, and level of education of the community. Today, corporations from American Airlines to Xerox use census data to shape their marketing strategies. Burger King, McDonald's, and Wendy's pore over census data to determine potential sites for their new fast-food franchises. Political organizations run the data through their computers to seek voters and contributors. The federal government uses census data to apportion revenue sharing funds.

Churches have also become major users of census data. From starting a new congregation to establishing a long-range plan for an existing church, demographic information is invaluable. This same information is vital to Christian public speakers, especially as they seek to learn the needs of their target audience.

The demographics of a community can be gathered from multiple sources. Though it is tedious, you may do a personal search through your local library, municipality, or chamber of commerce. Your denomination may have access to such information and can provide you with their findings. Several demographic services can produce as much information as you would like. The critical information you need to obtain regarding your community is as follows:

- *Population.* How many people live within a fifteen-minute drive of your church? How much has the population increased or declined in the last five years? How do these statistics compare with the national average?
- *Age.* The age structure is one of the most important variables

in understanding the characteristics of population. What
is the median age of the community where your church is
located? What percentage of the population is below the
age of eighteen? What percentage is between the ages of
twenty-five to forty-five? What percentage is between the
ages of forty-five to sixty-five? What percentage is age sixty-
five or older? How do these facts compare with the nation's
population?

- *Race.* The concept of race reflects self-classification by individuals according to the class or kind of people with
which they most closely identify. Nationally, the distribution of racial categories is as follows: (1) white—80.3 percent; (2) black—12.1 percent; (3) American Indian,
Eskimo, or Aleut—0.8 percent; (4) Asian or Pacific Islander—2.9 percent; and (5) other races—3.9 percent.[4]
What are the distribution of racial categories in your community? (1) White? (2) Black? (3) American Indian, Eskimo, or Aleut? (4) Asian or Pacific Islander? (5) Other?
Note: Hispanic origin is not a racial category. Persons of
Hispanic origin are those who classify themselves in one
of the following categories: Mexican, Puerto Rican, Cu-
ban, or other Spanish/Hispanic origin. Nationally, 52 percent of Hispanics identify themselves as white, while 42
percent identify themselves racially as "other."

- *Households.* There are two types of households: family and
nonfamily. A family consists of a householder and one or
more additional persons living in the same domestic unit
who are related to the householder by birth, marriage, or
adoption. A nonfamily household is an individual living
alone or with other non-related individuals. How
many family households live in your community? How
many nonfamily households live in your community?
How many family households have individuals married
without children? Married with children? How many
single-parent families? How many persons living alone?
What is the average household size in your community?

- *Housing.* Nationally, 58 percent of all housing units are occupied by owners, while 32 percent are occupied by renters.[5] How do these facts compare with what is true in your community? What percentage of all housing units is occupied by owners? What percentage is occupied by renters?
- *Household Income.* What is the average household income for your community? What is the percentage of people living in poverty in your community? What percentage of families have a dual income?
- *Educational Attainment.* Educational attainment is reported for persons age twenty-five and older and is usually associated with income. What percentage of your community's population has completed high school? How many have graduated from college? Of the college graduates, what percentage have a graduate degree?
- *Mobility.* The mobility of an area is determined by comparing one's place of residence in one year with their place of residence five years later. Stable areas are those where the persons live in the same house in the current year as they did five years ago. What percentage of the population lived in the same house this year as they did five years ago? What percentage lived in a different place of residence?
- *Transportation and Travel to Work.* What is the average number of vehicles available to each household in your community? How do people travel to work? What is the percentage who drive alone to work? How many carpooled? How many take public transportation (for instance, train, bus, subway, and so on)? What was the number of people and the time it took them to get to work? Less than ten minutes? Ten to thirty minutes? Thirty to sixty minutes? More than sixty minutes? What time did residents leave for work? What percentage left before 7 A.M.? What percentage left between 7 A.M. and 8 A.M.? What percentage left between 8 A.M. and 9 A.M.? What percentage work shift hours?
- *Employment.* Of the number of people employed, what kinds of work did the majority of them have? Retail trade?

Finance, insurance, or real estate? Management or executive? Professional? Sales? Clerical? Agricultural? Manufacturing? Entertainment/recreational services? Educational? Technical? Labor?

PSYCHOGRAPHICS

Psychographics investigates those issues that people value, what they feel is important, and what they think about certain topics and themes. In other words, psychographics gives the mental and emotional makeup of individuals in terms of their personality, attitude, mind-set, and lifestyle. These "soft" data are emerging as important types of information for knowing one's culture.

While the business world has used this information for years, the church has employed it even longer. Especially in Christian missionary endeavors, strategists were identifying the differences between cultures. No missionary to a foreign country would try to evangelize and to minister to people without first understanding their culture. Likewise, in today's multicultural environments, it is just as important for Christian public communicators to understand the cultural milieu of their target audience. Rick Warren, in *The Purpose-Driven Church,* wrote, "We don't have to agree with our culture, but we *must* understand it."[6]

There are several ways to gather this information. A variety of companies can provide it for you and your church. This information will identify the distinctive consumer groups and classify your neighborhoods into types, or market segments, through the statistical technique of cluster analysis.[7]

For example, I have discovered that my community falls into basically two groups: affluent families and up-and-coming singles. But from those groups there are four distinct types that further describe my ministry context: prosperous baby boomers, successful suburbanites, enterprising young singles, and semirural lifestyle.

A psychographic report will provide a description for each group of people. I can learn more about the people in my ministry context by understanding each distinct type. For example, in examining but one group—the prosperous baby boomers—I learned the following about them:

> [They] are a group that sets the trend for working wives, especially families with working mothers. They are described as follows: Prosperous baby boomers pursue an active lifestyle through participation in sports, especially court sports like tennis or racquetball, civic groups, and adult education. They drive minivans and 4x4 vehicles and undertake home projects. Expenditures include electronics, camcorders, PCs, sports equipment, home furnishings, and children paraphernalia. Television viewing is below average; magazine reading (metropolitan and business/finance) is above average. They do not invest or save in proportion to their income, but they do carry a lot of insurance. The study reports that the age profile of this market is unusual: baby boomers aged 25–44 years with young, primarily preschool children. These families are very mobile; over 35 percent of the population have moved in the past five years, which is double the national mobility rates. Their high income is a result of two salaries. Two-thirds have attended college or completed a degree. More than three-quarters of this market segment own homes in new housing developments. Primarily suburban, their neighborhoods are located within commuting distance of metropolitan job centers.[8]

Information such as this becomes extremely valuable in bringing your target audience into focus. These data paint a picture of the people that make up the community you serve. This information becomes crucial in selecting the topics and illustrations you use in your public speaking.

PNEUMAGRAPHICS

The third area of investigation is determining what I call "pneumagraphics" of a community. This information constitutes the "spiritual" data of an area. The spiritual background, which incorporates one's religious beliefs and church experiences, further defines the target. This information will help you to determine where God is already at work in your community. Since we are about kingdom business, these data will help us fit our efforts with those of other churches and ministries.

Questions to ask to determine the religious makeup of the community include the following: How many churches are in your ministry area? What are the predominate denominations or religious affiliations? What is the membership of the ten largest churches in your area? What are the ministry strengths of these churches? What are the ministry areas that seem not to be addressed by churches in your community? Where do you sense that the hand of God is currently working among churches or church-related ministries in your community? Are there other religious bodies in your community where there influence is felt? (These might include the Mormons, Jehovah's Witnesses, and other unorthodox groups.) What are the religious institutions and Christian ministries that influence your area?

Networking with other pastors and ministry leaders will disclose much information about the spiritual climate of your community. I would strongly encourage you to make appointments with various pastors in your neighborhood, especially those who have a lengthy tenure, to discuss the spiritual and emotional needs of the people in your ministry context. Other service professionals (such as school guidance counselors, pastoral counselors, police personnel, and hospital chaplains) can give you insight into the needs of your community.

In a discussion about the spirituality of an area, one cannot overlook the presence of mega churches and other religious institutions (such as schools, colleges, and seminaries). For example, my church is located in a Chicago suburb. I cannot overlook the influence of Willow Creek Community Church in South Barrington, especially with its strong "seeker-orientated" philosophy. I also cannot overlook the fact that Naperville sits on the fringe of the "mini-Bible belt" of Wheaton, especially with

Wheaton College and many parachurch ministries located close by. Likewise, the presence of Moody Bible Institute is felt.

THE PROFILE

Once you gather the information mentioned previously, a profile of the typical residents will emerge. These are the people your church is trying to reach. They may even be some of the people who are coming to your church to hear you preach and teach. Consider this question: "If we don't know *who* we are trying to reach, *how* will we ever know how to reach them?" Here's the follow-up question: "If we don't know *who* is in our listening audience, *how* will we know whether we have spoken to his or her needs?"

Once I had gathered the vital information related to my community, a general profile of the typical residents in Naperville began to emerge. I called them "Naperville Norman and Nancy." They have the following characteristics:

- They have a family.
- They own their own home and spend extra money to refurnish and remodel it.
- They are highly educated and value education for their children.
- They are upwardly mobile.
- They have little discretionary time.
- They are professionals in managerial or technological jobs that force them to travel frequently.
- They work hard.
- They play hard at golf, tennis, or racquetball.
- They make a tremendous amount of money but have equally substantial credit card and consumer debt.
- They are active in civic clubs and neighborhood groups.
- They read often.
- They have all the latest electronic gadgets.
- They are ambitious.
- They value quality of life.

- They drive a minivan and four-wheel-drive vehicles.
- They are high achievers and goal-oriented.
- They are materialistic.
- They are teetering on burnout.
- They struggle to have quality relationships.

The above information clarifies what is in the mind and on the heart of the typical residents in my community. I can see what is most important to their calendars and pocketbooks. The data educate me about their values and desires. The information opens a window so that I can look inside their world, hear their thoughts, and share their dreams.

As I begin to understand these characteristics, the features of "Naperville Norman and Nancy" also begin to come into focus for me. Nevertheless, I still know them only from a distance. They are my neighbors down the street. I see them but not every day. I know what they drive, but I don't know whether the interior of their vehicles is leather or cloth. I know they care about their lawn and house appearance, but I don't know the style of furniture they own. I see them playing with their kids, but I don't know how they discipline them. I know that they go to work early and come home late, but I don't know their specific job assignments. I know that their companies transferred them here a couple of years ago and that they will probably leave in a year or two, but I don't know where they will go or how they feel about it. I know that they like to play golf every Saturday morning, but I don't know whether any of their golfing partners constitute quality relationships.

As you can see, the picture of our target audience is still fuzzy. In order to make our aim more accurate, we must move from understanding the cultural values and assumptions of our listeners to profiling the community in which they live. Doing this will not only inform our Christian public speaking but will also give us a sharper image at which to take aim (the subject of the next chapter).

ENDNOTES

1. Lee Strobel, *Inside the Mind of Unchurched Harry and Mary* (Grand Rapids: Zondervan, 1993), 162.
2. Doug Murren, *The Baby Boomerang* (Ventura, Calif.: Regal, 1990), 191.
3. George Barna, *Marketing the Church* (Colorado Springs: NavPress, 1988), 26.
4. "HMB 1990 Census Guide Research Report" (Atlanta: Home Mission Board, Southern Baptist Convention), 7.
5. Ibid., 12.
6. Rick Warren, *The Purpose-Driven Church* (Grand Rapids: Zondervan, 1995), 165.
7. ACORN: Consumer Classification System, User's Guide (Arlington, Va.: CACI Marketing Systems, 1994), 5.
8. Ibid., 22.

CHAPTER FIVE

TAKING AIM AT THE TARGET AUDIENCE

*Preaching that costs nothing
accomplishes nothing.*
—John Henry Jowett

The target audience comes into focus by knowing and understanding the community. It's true that the church meets in a building and is often associated with a structure. But the congregation is made up of people whom God has brought together to carry out His purposes in a particular location. In order for the church to fulfill its God-given mandate, it must make use of staff, both paid and volunteer, to implement its programs, provide its ministries, and promote its cause. The congregation reflects a wide assortment of people with varied backgrounds, unique gifts, and differing strengths and weaknesses.

To be effective communicators, Christian public speakers must evaluate the nature of the people in their audience. To illustrate my point, consider the typical football coach. Prior to the start of the season, he tries to determine the talent and skill level of his players in order to design an offensive and defensive strategy that will give him the greatest likelihood of winning. The coach will drill and scrimmage the players in order to produce not only effective play but also to spot potential weaknesses and needs. Once he has identified these areas of concern, he can give the proper training and education to overcome them.

Likewise, Christian public speakers need to evaluate the make-up of the people in their audience (for example, a church) in order to identify areas of concern, weakness, and potential danger. This task is especially called for in a congregation that operates in a highly transitional community. This assessment will define and characterize the target audience by providing "the portrait of the persons to be addressed in the sermon."[1]

Effective public speaking becomes personal to your audience when you directly address different kinds of hearers and shape the content of your message to meet their specific needs. If you don't target the message toward the people who make up your audience and shape the application to fit their needs and concerns, they will tune you out. If our messages are not directed with pinpoint accuracy, we will fail to connect with our listeners. Television has practiced this targeting principle for so long that our audiences are accustomed to it. When they attend a Christian public gathering (such as Sunday morning worship at church), they expect (whether consciously or unconsciously) that the speaker will address their personal concerns.

How much do you know about the people in your audience? This question reminds me of the little poem that Peter Marshall once wrote:

> We have the nicest garbage man.
> He empties out our garbage can.
> He's just as nice as he can be.
> He always stops and talks to me.
> My mother doesn't like his smell.
> But mother doesn't know him well.

Since knowing your target audience and having an direct impact on them increase in direct proportion to each other, being intimately aware of their needs is crucial to the success of your public speaking ministry. As John Maxwell writes, "You can impress people from a distance, but you impact them close up."[2]

If you are like me after reading this, you're now incorporating the "YBH" principle—Yes But How? Later on in this chapter I provide several ways that you can gather these data so that you can know your target audience better. The main way is simply to ask them for the information you need about them. This can be done by surveying the target audience to discover their hopes and disappointments and their failures and successes. But before we undertake that process, there is a series of questions related to the demographic make-up of your church that you should consider.

THE CHURCH MEMBERSHIP DEMOGRAPHICS

Just as a community has demographics, so does a church. When one knows the demographics of the congregation, that information can be compared to the demographics of the community. This will enable you to take better aim at your target audience and be more relevant in your public speaking. These data will also help you determine whether the church is reaching the typical resident of its community. The demographics of your church can be identified by asking the same sorts of questions that you asked about your community.

- *Population.* What is the resident membership of your church? How many regular attenders would call your congregation their church home? How many prospects have attended your church in the past year, but have not joined or affiliated with the congregation? What percentage of the community is your church reaching?
- *Age.* What is the median age of your church? What percentage of the membership is below the age of eighteen? What percentage is the age of nineteen to twenty-five? What percentage is the age of twenty-five to forty-five? What percentage is the age of forty-five to sixty-five? What percentage is the age of sixty-five or older?

- *Race.* What is the racial distribution of your church population? White? Black? Asian? Something else?
- *Households.* What percentage of your church population lives in family households? What percentage lives in nonfamily households? What is the breakdown of households that are married without children? What percentage is married with children? What percentage is single parent families? What percentage have persons living alone?
- *Housing.* What percentage of families in your church owns their own home? What percentage is renting? How does this information compare with the national and local averages?
- *Educational Attainment.* What percentage of the people in your target audience has completed high school? How many have graduated from college? What percentage has received graduate degrees?
- *Mobility.* What percentage of the church membership is living at the same address as five years ago? What percentage has moved to your community within the last five years? What percentage will not be moving from their present residence? What percentage will move at some time in the future? Of those moving at some time in the future, what percentage will move within the next five years? How many times has the adult population of your church moved in their adult life?
- *Employment.* Where do your church members work? What percentage are professionals? Managerial or executive? Finance/insurance/real estate? Technological? Sales? Clerical? What are some other descriptions that would fit your community and church profile?

The next step is for you to examine thoroughly the information you gather. What do these data say about your church community? What are they thinking? What are they feeling? Where do faith issues intersect with these people? What are their values? Dreams? Hopes? Fears? What mental picture of the people in your church can you draw from this information?

THE CHURCH MEMBERSHIP QUESTIONNAIRE

The following is a demographic and personal needs questionnaire to clarify further the target audience and save you time in gathering information about them. This tool will allow the Christian public speaker and other church leaders to evaluate the demographic information and the most pressing needs of the target audience. If you use this tool wisely, it will help you to take aim at your target audience.

I have discovered that asking my congregation to complete this survey every two years gives me a good reading on their needs and concerns. If you give the survey too often, your target audience will grow tired and weary of it. In contrast, if you don't give the survey often enough, you will not have an accurate picture of the prevailing issues that are paramount in the lives of your constituents.

The Questionnaire

I suggest having the adult segment of your congregation complete the survey at the beginning of the Bible study classes or small group meetings. The form can be completed at any time (for instance, before or after small group meetings, before the worship hour, or after being received in the mail). The best results, however, will come when the respondents are given fifteen minutes to complete the survey and are asked to return the form immediately.

If the questionnaire is given during a programmed event (such as Bible study or Sunday morning worship), the group leader should say the following:

> The leadership of our church is interested in ministering to us and our needs more effectively. In order to do this, they must have our input. That's why they have asked us to complete the questionnaire you have in your hands. Everyone should have a survey. Is there anyone who didn't get one? Our responses will be scored and the results will be reviewed by our church leadership. Your responses to the survey will remain confidential. No one will know what

you marked on your survey. Please indicate how often the numbered statements on the survey are true of you: "Always," "Often," "Sometimes," "Seldom," or "Never." Please fill in only one answer per statement. If you change your answer, be sure that you completely erase your first mark. We will take the next fifteen minutes to complete this survey before we move on to the rest of our meeting.

CHURCH MEMBERSHIP QUESTIONNAIRE

Your responses to this survey will remain confidential. No one will know what you have marked. This information will be used to assist our pastor and church leadership in meeting the needs of this congregation. Thank you for your cooperation.

PART A—MEMBERSHIP PROFILE

1. **Gender:**
   ___ 1) Male   ___ 2) Female

2. **Age:**
   ___ 1) 18–22
   ___ 2) 23–29
   ___ 3) 30–44
   ___ 4) 45–64
   ___ 5) 65 and above

3. **Race:**
   ___ White ___ Black ___ Asian ___ Other

4. **Marital Status:**
   ___ 1) Single
   ___ 2) Married
   ___ 3) Separated
   ___ 4) Widowed
   ___ 5) Divorced

5. **Housing:**
   ___ Buying ___ Renting ___ Other

6. **Education:**

   ___ High School ___ College ___ Graduate School

7. **How long has your family lived at your present address?**

   ___ 1) Less that five years ___ 2) More than five years

8. **Transportation to Work:**

   Average travel time to work _____

9. **Employment:**

   Identify your occupation _____

PART B—SURVEY OF PERSONAL NEEDS

Tell how frequently these statements are true of you. Please mark the line with an *A* for "Always," *B* for "Often," *C* for "Sometimes," *D* for "Seldom," and *E* for "Never," or *N/A* for "Not Applicable." Please indicate only one answer per statement.

___ 1) I have feelings of insecurity.

___ 2) I worry about debt.

___ 3) I have a satisfying marriage.

___ 4) I think about the future.

___ 5) I feel as if my family has no roots.

___ 6) I feel that I don't understand the Bible.

___ 7) I welcome new friendships.

___ 8) I wonder whether my children will experience a quality of life similar to the one I have.

___ 9) I welcome change.

___ 10) I feel the pressure of many time constraints.

___ 11) I have plenty of friends.

___ 12) I think about making more money.

___ 13) My family lives with unresolved conflict.

___ 14) I wonder where I will live when I retire.

___ 15) I place high expectations on people.

___ 16) God does not seem to be there for me when things are going bad.

___ 17) I feel as if I don't know many people.

___ 18) My inconsistency in raising my children frustrates me.

___ 19) Change is difficult for me to handle.

___ 20) I can't be as committed to outside job pursuits as I would like.

___ 21) I wonder whether I will have enough money to be able to retire comfortably.

___ 22) I would change jobs to receive a higher salary.

___ 23) My loved ones and I have difficulty communicating easily and openly.

___ 24) I think about going "home."

___ 25) I feel lonely.

___ 26) I seek God's direction in making major changes in my life.

___ 27) I feel as if I don't have anyone to talk with about my struggles.

___ 28) My children adjust well to new environments.

___ 29) I wish life were more stable.

___ 30) I welcome a new job assignment so that I can spend more time with my family.

___ 31) I would relocate my family for a higher-paying job.

___ 32) I don't have a sense of purpose.

___ 33) I want to know the benefits of new church programs.

___ 34) I wish I knew God's will for my life.

___ 35) I open up easily to new people.

___ 36) Relocating is harmful to my family's well being.

___ 37) I become restless after living in one place for a while.

___ 38) I feel the stress of overcommitment.

___ 39) My present job has an uncertain future.

___ 40) I worry about my aging parents.

___ 41) I feel used by my employer.

___ 42) I wonder whether God cares where I work or live.

___ 43) I place my family over my career.

___ 44) I have difficulty maintaining relationships.

___ 45) The Bible doesn't seem to offer solutions to the problems in my life.

Purpose

This survey is designed to identify the needs of the adult population in a highly mobile target audience. The survey asks for certain demographic information and responses to a series of need-related statements. It attempts to bring the Christian public speaker closer to the heart, mind, and soul of the people in the target audience. It seeks to assist the communicator in planning for messages and to provide data concerning the listeners.

Respondents disclose certain demographic information. For instance, Part A of the form asks questions that are specific to their needs. In Part B, respondents indicate whether a statement is true of them "always," "often," "sometimes," "seldom," or "never." As such, this survey is similar to an opinion poll, for it relates what people report about themselves. The questionnaire does not identify personal traits, assign cause-and-effect relationships, apply to the whole target audience, or give predictions about future behaviors. But it does provide a snapshot of what people are saying that they feel is true about them.

Generally speaking, areas of need are identified by statements that receive responses of "sometimes," "often," or "always." Dominant areas of need are represented by responses of "often" or "always." These areas are likely to influence decisions, behavior, thought life, and relationships. Moderate areas of need are represented by responses of "sometimes." These areas may influence people's thoughts and actions, especially in stressful circumstances.

Assumptions

The basis of this survey grew out of my many years of ministry in highly transitional settings. Pastoral contacts, counseling sessions, and personal visits with people in a state of transition or major change over the years have disclosed several recurring themes. These are pressure points that tend to intensify when they go unresolved. The typical Naperville resident profile also raised other issues that should be questioned. For instance, would the characteristics of "Naperville Norman and Nancy" be true of people congregating at Naperville Baptist Church?

The statements in the questionnaire are based on several assumptions. For example, people move frequently because of economic and employment reasons. Until they reach a certain level in their professional life, their security tends to be fragile. Because corporate management moves often, those people tend to keep one eye on the horizon of tomorrow. Relationships among frequent movers are few, shallow, and difficult to initiate and maintain. Yet for these people change is easy and often welcomed.

Furthermore, people in the upper socioeconomic levels tend to place higher value on education, status, money, family, time, and quality of life. These values, however, do not come without a price. There is more time spent in school before entering the job force, residing in communities with a higher cost of living to guarantee better schools and status, longer work days to make more money and ensure greater security, less time spent with spouse and children, and greater expectations about attaining personal goals. When all of these factors are taken into consideration, the following needs are questioned.

Needs Questioned

This survey is designed to address the general felt needs of a local church and the target audience's specific concerns related to mobility. The following issues are appraised.

- *Job Security Issues* (statements 1, 11, 21, 31, 39). Everyone wants security in life. With the "downsizing," "rightsizing," and potentially "capsizing" of modern corporations, this issue is the topic of water fountain conversations.
- *Financial Issues* (statements 2, 12, 22). Closely related to the job security issue is financial concern. With the busters and boomers wondering whether "they will ever have enough money," what degree of influence will financial matters have on an individual's life?
- *Family Issues* (statements 3, 8, 13, 18, 23, 28, 36, 40, 43). Although almost every question in the survey touches upon

family life, to some degree certain statements specifically measure people's perceptions about their family life.

- *Future Concerns* (statements 4, 14, 24, 32). Thoughts about future activities can and do affect behavior; therefore, statements tend to be made about one's perception of the future.
- *Emotional Issues* (statements 5, 15, 25, 33, 41). A brief reading of the Psalms indicates that people's emotions play a vital role in their relationship with God. Yet the wrong emphasis is often placed upon these emotions by either totally ignoring them or overly depending upon them. Certain statements deal at face value with some of the major emotions in people's lives.
- *Spiritual Issues* (statements 6, 16, 26, 34, 42, 45). Like family issues, spiritual issues cannot be separated from the rest of one's life. However, a Christian public speaker needs to question the feelings of the target audience about the Bible and God's involvement in their lives.
- *Relational Issues* (statements 7, 17, 27, 35). Relationships are a huge part of life. We need them to remain healthy. What are the perceptions of your target audience concerning their relational involvement with others?
- *Responses to Change* (statements 9, 19, 29, 37). "The only thing constant is change," the old saying goes. One's adaptation and positive response to change can affect mental and emotional health.
- *Time Availability* (statements 10, 20, 30, 38). The target audience's perception of available time and its influence on their quality of life needs to be known.

ASSESSMENT OF THE QUESTIONNAIRE

Once your target audience has completed the questionnaire, you should compile the information in a single report. Although doing this is tedious, simply adding the responses from each statement and averaging the information will give you the appropriate data for each demographic question and for each need-based statement.

You can then gather further data by determining the responses according to each demographic statement.

Once this assessment is done, you will have a picture of the target audience as a whole. If a further delineation of the information is desired, you can have the needs of males, females, marrieds, and singles denoted for each possible demographic question you ask.

- *Dominant Needs*. The statements that indicate a dominant level of concern are denoted by the responses of "always" or "often." What were the four most frequently cited needs among the respondents?
- *Moderate Needs*. Statements that indicate a moderate level of concern have a total of over 70 percent when the responses of "always," "often," and "sometimes" are combined.
- *Cluster of Issues*. When the responses are tabulated according to the cluster of statements pertaining to each major issue, what issues are the greatest areas of need? What did the security issues disclose? Financial issues? Family issues? Future concerns? Emotional issues? Spiritual issues? Relational issues? Responses to change? Time availability? You can obtain this information by averaging the responses to the statements related to each particular cluster issue.
- *Demographic Assessment*. An assessment of the survey based on the demographic information requested will disclose information about your church.
- *Gender*. Did the men and women surveyed disclose similar concerns? How were their concerns different? What were the needs and concerns of the males? Of the females?
- *Age*. What did the various age groups identify as their concerns? As their needs? As their issues? What did the respondents disclose, especially when grouped according to living at their present address for less than five years and more than five years?
- *Theological Assessment*. As I listen to the comments of

people in my target audience and as I analyze the data I have gathered in this study, I am able to make some assessments regarding their spiritual longings. Once I had completed the study of my target audience and deciphered their responses to the questionnaire, I had exegeted my listeners. I had a better understanding of who they are and where they are going. As I evaluated my target audience, I was able to make the following theological assessment:

Spiritually, there is a hunger within my target audience to know God and His plans for their lives. Many, if not most, know that God is (or at least should be) the reason for their existence. They know that the Lord should be the driving force and controlling center of their lives. And while most are secure in their knowledge of eternal life, they are less secure in finding meaning in their temporal life. While they have a relationship with God, there is a hunger and void for deeper meaning and greater intimacy with Him.

In an effort to find God's way of life, the members of my target audience have substituted the pursuit of the "good life" for an intimate relationship with Him. Correspondingly, there exists within them an element of guilt and frustration. There is a deep sense of knowing what is right and godly, yet choosing an alternate worldly path to fill the innermost hunger. Consequently, my listeners are filled with depression and loneliness. Since they are trusting in themselves more than God, insecurity creeps into their lives.

A clash of values wages within the members of my target audience. On the one hand, they desire to enjoy what their neighbors and coworkers have in terms of affluence and prestige. Yet, on the other hand, the possibility of unethical business practices and a failure to spend appropriate time with their family tempts my listeners to adopt worldly standards. As a result, they sometimes leave behind (or completely abandon) biblical values.

While rootlessness has resulted from mobility, restlessness has resulted from rootlessness. Many of the people in my target audience are not happy. They wear their smiles in public but remove them like their coats when they return to the privacy of their homes. They want more, think that they need more, and consequently aspire to have more—whether it is more time, more possessions, more money, or more prestige. But like a drug addict, their increased wealth gives a momentary high that soon dissipates.

For the most part the people in my target audience are biblically literate. They have been grounded in the Scriptures. But they are practical atheists. While they believe what the Bible teaches, they do not read it. They feel strongly about the church and its traditions, but they are unfaithful and inconsistent in attending corporate worship. They know about God, but they do not consult Him on every issue facing them or their family. They have a strong desire for community service and a heart for justice, but they have little time to get involved.

One should always guard against interpreting every action, thought, and behavior from one's narrow perspective, even a theological point of view. It is like the old saying, "If one only has a hammer, then every problem is treated like a nail." I don't want to read into the questionnaires and demographic information more than what actually exists. Yet the pervasive mood among the members of my target audience seems to be that of emptiness, despite having so much, including some sort of relationship with God.

By knowing this information and making the necessary assessment, I am now in a much better position to pinpoint my messages (both their content and application) so that I can address the needs of my listeners where they are living.

THE PROFILE OF "NAPERVILLE
BAPTIST CHURCH NORM AND NAN"

By now my target audience is coming into sharper focus. After going through the process discussed above, I was able to further delineate my listeners. My target audience is the typical attender of Naperville Baptist Church. I will call them "Naperville Baptist Church Norm and Nan." They are not vastly different from "Naperville Norman and Nancy." But they are different in some ways. "Norm and Nan" have the following characteristics:

- They have a young family.
- They own their own home.
- They are educated and value education for their children.
- They are extremely mobile.
- They are pressured by too little time for the things they deem important.
- They are professionals in sales, managerial, or technological jobs.
- They play golf.
- They are concerned about the future and want to know God's will for their lives.
- They are stressed by an overcommitted lifestyle at work, at home and at church.
- Money is important to them but not to the detriment of children and family.
- Their expectations of people—even people at church, especially leaders—are high.
- They worry about both the immediate and the extended family.
- They drive a minivan and a company car.
- They are more concerned for their family's well-being than about their present job.

When I compared this information with the Naperville Norman and Nancy profile, I discovered that a slightly different picture began to emerge. It is the difference between a photograph in focus and one slightly out of focus. Or better yet, it is the difference between standing far away from a work of art and standing up close to it. By standing far away, one can still see the picture and make some sense of it. But by standing close to the artwork, one begins to see the rich hues and textures of the painting. When up close, the onlooker can now say, "Oh, I get it!"

By understanding the characteristics of your target audience, you will be better able to take aim at the heart, mind, and soul of your listeners. By profiling both the typical community resident and the church resident, your messages will not only be generally focused but also specifically targeted. You will move from a factual knowledge of your target audience to an experiential understanding of them, which is imperative as you seek to communicate to their needs.

Now that we have taken aim at our target audience, we next must lock onto them. As we will discover in the next chapter, this involves contrasting and compiling the information we gathered in our questionnaire to determine how we should specifically develop our messages.

ENDNOTES

1. Fred B. Craddock, *Preaching* (Nashville: Abingdon, 1985), 87.
2. John Maxwell, *Senior Pastor Profile* (San Diego: Injoy, 1996), 25.

CHAPTER SIX

LOCKING ONTO
THE TARGET AUDIENCE

*I preach as never sure to preach again, and as a
dying man to dying men.*
—Richard Baxter

Speed and precision. All-out, go-for-broke sprints followed by intense concentration—and a gentle squeeze on the trigger. No, it's not the busy public speaker's weekly routine, though there are enormous similarities. Instead, it's the biathlon, an athletic competition that combines cross-country skiing and rifle shooting. A biathlete must be able to strain to the physical limits, then immediately calm the body and slow the heartbeat to shoot a .22 caliber rifle (which he carries on his back while he skis) at small targets fifty meters away. When the biathlete is standing, the targets are 115 millimeters, which is slightly larger than a CD (compact disk). When the biathlete is prone (lying on his stomach), the target is forty-five millimeters, which is about the size of a silver dollar.

As a Christian public speaker, I often feel like a biathlete. I'm frequently racing through the week from one activity to another, and struggling to spend the necessary time to perform the needed duties of my job. But on Sunday morning I have to slow down, ease my heart rate, concentrate with tremendous intensity, and take aim at my target audience. I slowly and methodically squeeze the trigger of my message to hit the needs and expectations of my listeners.

While I have never competed in a biathlon, I think the task of Christian public speakers is greater in difficulty. I know that it has greater eternal consequences. If the biathlete misses his target, one minute for each miss is added to his overall event time. But if Christian public speakers miss their target, the eternal destiny of souls is at stake. The biathlete may miss his target and lose a medal. But when the Christian public speaker misses the target, a life could be lost forever to the kingdom of God.

I don't want to take that chance. I want to have the needs of my target audience in the cross-hairs of my message scope. In order for that to happen, I need to assess the information about my community and my listeners to determine the make-up of the latter. Doing this will enable me to lock onto them better. First, let's look at some masters of Christian public speaking who are worthy role models of this practice. These proclaimers of truth always hit their target audience with their message.

THE PROCLAIMERS OF TRUTH

Into each period of biblical history came messengers who proclaimed God's truth to needy people. These heralds hit their target audience like a champion biathlete. For all practical purposes, the spokespeople of biblical times can be grouped into two broad groups: Old Testament prophets and New Testament preachers. We can learn immensely from their example about how to lock onto our target audience.

Old Testament Prophets

Whatever one could say about the Old Testament prophets, one cannot deny that they were proclaimers of divine truth who had flare, courage, and dynamic qualities. They spoke to the political, social, and religious conditions of their time. These people of God provided an interpretation of history. They consistently displayed insight into the eternal purposes of God for

His people. Into each context they announced the eternal principles of divine providence.

These prophets spoke on behalf of God. While the idea of prediction was present in the word *prophet* throughout the Old Testament, these heralds were primarily messengers to their own age. They witnessed to the deeds and truths of God as much as they foretold the future. In other words, they were "forth" tellers even more than foretellers.

The prophets of God consistently showed themselves to be uncompromising individualists who were not bound by social conventions and public opinion. They were conscious of a divine call that held them to their God-given task. They had intimate communion with God, and this enabled them to bear His precious message to a spiritually impoverished people. These heralds kept in touch with the Lord through prayer. They were people of action who addressed the concerns of their listeners. The prophets of the Old Testament were outspoken critics of specific evils in society. Furthermore, they were God's agents to unveil His future plans for His people (as well as all humanity).

Into each new generation different prophets of God raced. At each stop along their course, they slowed their heart rate and spoke with boldness and conviction to their target audience. The prophets didn't just speak; they also thundered. They didn't just write moving messages; they also spoke for God. In fact, these heralds oftentimes were the message they proclaimed. They knew exactly where to aim their declarations, and they scored a direct hit every time.

New Testament Preachers

The preachers in the New Testament era were town criers, or heralds, who lifted up their voices and drew public attention to Christianity. They proclaimed truth and grace to both the Christian and the pagan alike. To the unbeliever, these divinely sent messengers presented the claims of the gospel in order to bring them to faith in Christ. To the believer, these heralds dealt with more pressing and complex spiritual matters. New Testament preachers dealt with theological and ethical problems that had arisen in the church. They sought to clarify the mind of God on a variety of controversial matters. In doing so, these early heralds declared how to conduct oneself in a godly manner in a pagan society.

The New Testament preachers also spoke on behalf of another. They sought to bring the eternal dimension of Christianity to a temporal need. For instance, their messages addressed the intellect, emotions, and will of their target audience to spur the listeners to become more Christlike.

These proclaimers of truth from bygone generations provide contemporary Christian public speakers proven models for delivering powerful and relevant messages. Hugh Thompson Kerr commented that "The New Testament is and always will be our best textbook on preaching."[1] "To return to apostolic preaching in our day would be to advance,"[2] J. B. Weatherspoon added. The students of New Testament preaching have at their disposal the most powerful and effective examples of the gospel message in history.

Let's examine three New Testament preachers who scored a direct hit on their target audience. The first person is Jesus. He proclaimed a message of redemption and salvation. In doing so, He consciously sought to identify the needs of His target audience. He accomplished this task either by questioning the individual or through keen observation.

The Savior was a communications specialist. George Barna contends, "He identified His target audience, determined their need, and delivered His message directly to them."[3] For instance, when Jesus encountered the woman at the well, He talked about water. When Christ spoke to Peter, the fisherman, He talked about fish. When Jesus conversed with a tax collector who had invited the Savior into his home, money became the topic of discussion. When Christ addressed a group of farmers, He spoke about the harvest. Jesus clearly targeted those living apart from God and crafted His approach accordingly.

Jesus scratched where people itched in His public speaking, and this enabled Him to lock onto His target audience. He began with their needs and interests and then moved them toward the truth. Though Jesus' messages were specific and relevant to His listeners, He did not allow them to define His agenda. He contextualized His message of redemption and grace so that it was pertinent to them.

Like a good teacher, Jesus started with the interests of His students and moved them toward the lesson He wanted to cover. Like a good salesperson, Christ started with the needs of the customers, not the product to be sold. Like a wise manager, Jesus began with the concerns of the employees, not His own agenda. He knew the exact location of His target audience, where they needed to go, and what He had to do to help them get there.

One can learn immensely from the methodology of Jesus. All Christian public speakers are wise to communicate spiritual truth by first discovering the needs of their target audience and then using this information as a starting point in their presentation. In this regard, Jesus still provides the best model for preaching.

The second example that I want to cite is the apostle Peter. He was able to proclaim God's truth in such a way that it was relevant to the culture milieu in which he lived. Peter was a believer with a message so compelling that he seized every opportunity to lock onto his target audience and score a direct hit with his proclamation. In every instance, the circumstance provided the point of contact that he needed with his listeners. F. J. Foakes-Jackson stated that it "cannot be disputed that [Peter's sermons] are wonderfully varied as to their character, and as a rule admirably suited to the occasion on which they were delivered."[4]

As a Christian public speaker, Peter was adroit enough to make what was of immediate interest to his audience the starting point of his messages. For instance, the sermons that he delivered on the Day of Pentecost and at Solomon's porch both began with a reference to some remarkable event that the onlookers failed to grasp. Peter's explanation of the underlying significance of the event became the basis for his extended discourse. Each message that he delivered was relevant to the situation at hand and pertinent to the target audience.

Peter bridged the gap between the Scriptures and his listeners. He knew God's Word, and he also knew the people whom he addressed. As a result, the apostle was highly effective and persuasive in his messages. Perhaps that is why Edgar Blake maintained, "Peter's sermon on the Day of Pentecost, measured by its results, immediate and remote, is undoubtedly the most effective Christian discourse ever delivered by a messenger of the cross."[5] In other words, Peter's preaching was appropriate to the context in which he spoke. His declarations were pertinent in their content, for he addressed people's needs with the truths of Christ. What Peter declared was relevant in its intent, for he led individuals to repentance and faith in the living Christ. The apostle's proclamations were appropriate in their authority, for his words were filled with God-given power. We can see why Peter's messages provide us with some of the finest examples of effective public speaking.

The third example that I want to cite is the apostle Paul. He did an amazing job of contextualizing his message to the needs of his target audience. Paul advocated speaking to people with words and reasoning they could understand. The apostle realized that the audience, not the messenger, was more important. Consequently, he was willing to shape his message to their needs in order to bring about a life-changing experience in their lives.

The sermon that Paul delivered in the synagogue in Pisidian Antioch is a fine example of missionary preaching. The address was marked by an appeal to the listeners. He demonstrated how ancient prophecies were fulfilled in the life of Christ. Paul declared that Jesus died for humanity's sins and offers forgiveness to all who believe in Him. Here was preaching eminently suited to the situation of the hearers. Paul began where people were, rooted his message in the history of Israel, and stressed the commonality that united both the proclaimer of God's truth and the target audience. The apostle showed the relevance and the fulfillment of the ancient Scriptures.[6] Michael Green noted that Paul's preaching was "intensely relevant, alike to the circumstances, concerns and consciences of the hearers."[7]

Paul personalized his messages by targeting them for specific audiences. For instance, note how the apostle did this in 1 Thessalonians 5:14: "And we urge you, brothers, warn those who are idle, encourage the timid, help the weak, be patient with everyone" (NIV). Here we find Paul cautioning the slothful, consoling the fearful, aiding the feeble, and remaining composed in his dealings with all sorts of people. The key to the apostle's pulpit ministry was sensitivity to others. He recognized the condition of each person and offered the appropriate remedy for each situation.

Jesus, Peter, and Paul made distinctive marks on their generation because they consistently locked onto their target audience and scored a direct hit with their messages. Their success was not by accident. They knew and understood the needs, aspirations, and concerns of their listeners. Christian public speakers today would do well to follow their example.

ASK THE RIGHT QUESTION

A key step in locking onto the target audience involves asking the right question. When the Barna Research Group asked unchurched people what might bring them into a church, the number one response (given by nearly one out of five) was better messages.[8] I suspect that what they meant by "better messages" was sermons that spoke to them where they lived and that addressed their pressing needs. People want Christian public speakers to know them personally, to empathize with their hurts, and to revel in their joys. Such messages are practical, for they teach people about daily living.

Rick Warren is the pastor of Saddleback Valley Community Church in Orange County, California. In the congregation's first fifteen years of existence—before it ever owned a building—it grew from one family to more than ten thousand in worship attendance. "Saddleback's fifteen years of growth," writes Warren, "in spite of hot gymnasiums, leaky tents, and crowded parking have shown that people will put up with a lot of inconveniences and limitations if the messages are genuinely meeting their needs."[9] Furthermore, he says that the message is still the most important element of the church's worship service.[10]

The inference from both Barna's national survey of the unchurched and the experience of Saddleback Valley Community Church is that if Christian public speakers ask the right question before preparing for their message, they will have a much better opportunity of locking onto their target audience. The question is not, What will I talk about? Rather, it is, To whom am I speaking? Knowing who makes up your target audience will help you to determine the content of your message. Such information will also enable your message to score a direct hit in the heart of your listeners.

Politicians have demonstrated the importance of correctly targeting audiences. They discovered (through methods that are similar to the ones I have discussed previously) the worries, fears, and hopes of their constituency. Politicians use this information to relate their dreams and goals to the concerns of their listeners.

Similarly, effective Christian public speakers make every effort to lock onto their target audience by preparing messages that will meet the needs of that particular group. I would be committing homiletical homicide if I presented the same message to a rural, southern church made up of mostly farmers as I would to my suburban, Midwestern church consisting of mostly professionals. A pastor of a church in a large metropolitan area who uses only rural illustrations should not be surprised to find urbanites unresponsive. The reverse is also true. The effective Christian public speaker is adept at understanding and knowing the educational, cultural, economic, ethnic, and religious makeup of his or her target audience and addressing them accordingly.

AIM AT THE RIGHT TARGET

The right question—"To whom am I speaking?"—implies that for the message to connect with the target audience, the homiletician must aim at the person sitting in the pew, not the neighbor living down the street. The Christian public speaker must move from focusing on the typical community resident to aiming at his or her listeners. That audience must be seen clearly in the scope of the orator's cross-hairs. It's true that on Sunday mornings one addresses a microcosm of the community. Knowing the neighborhood resident is a major first step in hitting the target with one's message. But the effective homiletician doesn't just want to "come close" or "be in the neighborhood." Rather, he or she wants to hit the bull's-eye dead center. Christian public speaking is not like a game of horseshoes or throwing hand grenades, where close is good enough. Instead, an effective pulpit ministry calls for pinpoint accuracy.

As a public speaker who strives to lock onto my target audience, I must move from knowing and understanding "Naperville Norman and Nancy" to addressing and speaking to "Naperville Baptist Church Norm and Nan." In other words, I must know my listeners as much as I know the biblical text. The church demographic information and questionnaire assessment pinpoints the aim of my messages and helps me to define my clientele. But like the Olympic biathlete gold medal winner who is separated from the silver medal winner by milliseconds, the differences between a listener and someone else in the community may differ only slightly.

How do the people sitting in my audience differ from those in my community? Not much, in my opinion. But pinpoint accuracy and "Gold Medal" messages demand that I know those subtle differences. Here's what I discovered.

"Naperville Baptist Church Norm and Nan" tend to be younger than their non-Christian counterparts. More of them have children and own their residence, and they have slightly more education than "Naperville Norman and Nancy." "Norm and Nan" are more mobile than the community resident. And they are more likely to be in financial, technological, or professional jobs than "Norman and Nancy." "Norm and Nan" have little discretionary time, and they spend their few precious moments with their family or at church.

This couple does not travel out of town as much as "Norman and Nancy." "Norm and Nan" play as much golf as "Norman and Nancy" but not as much tennis or racquetball. "Norm" is not as active in civic groups and clubs as "Norman and Nancy," but "Nan" is involved in a neighborhood group. Their family drives a minivan, while the second car is a company car, not a sports utility vehicle. They are not as materialistic as "Norman and Nancy," for they have been influenced by the practice of Christian stewardship. "Norm and Nan" are teetering on burn-out, with some of the strain coming from church involvement. They hunger to have quality relationships and are making small strides in that direction.

"Naperville Baptist Church Norm and Nan" are concerned about their future. They feel the pressure of too many time constraints. They are biblically based and seek to know God's will. They are interested in church, especially for the spiritual benefit of their children. But they want to know the value of participating in a specific program before they get involved. They place a high value on their family's quality of life. Yet this is undercut by the long hours they spend at the office. Their interest and concern for their loved ones goes beyond their immediate household to their extended family. This Christian couple is concerned about their aging parents, and they feel the strain of being many miles away from them.

The paramount concerns of "Naperville Baptist Church Norm and Nan" relate to their time, finances, and emotional well-being. In regard to time, they feel that they do not have enough of it to balance out their vocational and family demands. Financially they are strapped. While they are making more money than they ever did before in their lives, they do not seem to have enough to make ends meet. They are in debt because they spend a lot of money on their house and to support their materialistic lifestyle. They are also stressed about financing their children's education.

Emotionally "Naperville Baptist Church Norm and Nan" feel the anxiety of having few roots and fewer friends. It's no wonder they are lonely and rudderless. They feel used by their employer, and they think that the company could care less about them, their future, their family, and their emotional health. This couple would gladly accept a job change that would give them additional time to spend with their loved ones and enable them to focus on being personally rejuvenated and refreshed.

Getting a fix on the consumer in your target audience is not as difficult as it may initially seem. Once you have gathered the information about the residents of the community and the people who listen to your messages, compare and contrast the two groups. The following are some of the questions you can ask to help you discover the similarities and differences. How do your listeners differ from the community residents:

- Educationally?
- Professionally?
- In time spent with family? Work? Civic activities? Recreation?
- In their travel and vacation plans?
- In the automobiles they drive?
- In sources of pressure and stress?
- In their knowledge of the Bible?
- In concerns about the church and church programs?
- In their values and convictions?
- With their family issues?
- Financially?
- In regard to debt?
- In future concerns and pursuits?
- In what they think that they are missing in their lives?
- Vocationally?
- In where they need relief?
- Socially?

THE UNDERLYING DESIRE OF EVERY CONSUMER

People in transient areas tend to move around quite often. They thus find it difficult to sustain intensive friendships and bonds with other people. They're on the move so much that they seem to have no time to share with others, much less care for others. It's no wonder that sociologist Vance Packard writes, "Rootlessness seems clearly to be associated with a decline in companionship, a decline in satisfying group activities, a decline in mutual trust, and a decline in psychological security. It encourages a shallowness in personal relationships and a relative indifference to community problems."[11]

The increasing mobility of our society has contributed to the feelings of loneliness and even isolation that people experience. Change means separation from family and friends, and a loss of the warm feelings of acceptance, predictability, and protection that loved ones give people. In times of separation these losses can produce anxiety, which in turn provokes anger, guilt, and insecurity. Such losses can only be met in and through developing new relationships.

If people going through such changes fail to recognize their deep-seated need for community, they will not be whole, healthy, or happy individuals. A church that values community is a place where people can feel that they belong, and where they can feel welcomed, accepted, challenged, and encouraged. An effective public speaker can move target audiences to develop a strong and healthy environment that will enrich their individual and collective lives. And a powerful communicator can also motivate people to reach out to others with the love and concern of Christ.

Christian public speaking can interpret the life change of biblical and contemporary stories and make applications that will help the listeners discover their need for others. Messages delivered from the pulpit can challenge the target audience to establish a network of supportive friends and ties in their new-found location. Of course, there are limitations to the teaching ministry of the church. While the speaker can encourage, interpret, and challenge the hearers to take appropriate actions, he or she cannot do the work for them. Nevertheless, the audience's desire for community needs to be addressed over and over again. If homileticians fail to speak to this issue, they will miss the target of one of the most glaring and often silent needs in the life of a congregation, especially a mobile one.

Public speaking that motivates people toward community can meander down many paths. Discussing and developing the themes related to the symbols of community is one such path. These symbols (such as communion and baptism) need to be explained not only for their sacramental value but also for their underlying essence for a people of faith. Teaching the analogies and metaphors of the church in the New Testament can be helpful, too. These graphic visual images (such as the church being a body, a fellowship, the temple of God, a holy nation, a flock, and a family) foster in the congregation the need for community. Reminding the people that salvation implies community is another way to promote fellowship among parishioners.

The Bible knows no salvation in isolation. Following Christ without banding with His people is a misnomer. That's why public speakers should recount stories of the church's past in order to develop a deep sense of camaraderie within the target audience regarding their unique traditions and heritages. To explain and develop community stories that are found in the Bible (such as the Exodus wanderings, the Israelites in captivity, the relationship of Jesus to His disciples, and the unity of believers in the face of opposition and tragedy) will play an important role in developing community life.

Jean Vanier writes, "Community life isn't simply created by either spontaneity or laws. It needs a certain discipline and particular forms of nourishment."[12] Public speaking can provide the nourishment for community to take place within the church. During times of transition, the target audience will be more aware of the need for community. A savvy communicator will seize the opportunity to address the listeners' needs. People in crisis—regardless of their status in life—will be ready to receive new insights and encouragement. Ministers should be aware of such times and understand the personal needs of their target audience. They should also have the ability to interpret Scripture properly. With this winning combination, they will be successful in explaining how the church can provide fellowship and support for those who hunger for community.

It's imperative to remember that Christian community is a means, not an end in itself. The mission of the church is to reach people for Christ, and community exists for the sake of that mission. The congregation that merely gathers to serve itself may feel like a nice place to socialize, but it is not furthering the kingdom of God. The church finds its true sense of community in following Jesus. People may want the church to provide only a safe haven from a vicious world. But Jesus has called us to discipleship in a Christian community context so that we can reach out to the world with His saving message.

THE PREACHER'S NEW ROLE

When the above practices and focus on community are emphasized through the speaker's messages, the perceptions of the target audience will change. They will feel differently about not only themselves but also the homiletician. They will welcome and applaud the fact that the minister knows their needs, interests, and concerns. In their minds he or she has moved from the role of a guest speaker who gropes to locate the target to that of an expert communicator who can zero in on the mark. Such an individual scores a direct hit every time he or she delivers a message.

Effective public speakers regard the target audience as more than a collection of people. They are seen as a fellowship of believers who worship the same Lord and care deeply for each other. Such a congregation is blessed to have homileticians who can both lock onto their needs through effective public speaking and fire the right arrow to hit the bull's-eye at dead center.

ENDNOTES

1. Hugh Thompson Kerr, *Preaching in the Early Church* (New York: Revell, 1942), 13.
2. Jessie Burton Weatherspoon, *Sent Forth to Preach: Studies in Apostolic Preaching* (New York: Harper and Brothers, 1954), 30.
3. George Barna, *Marketing the Church* (Colorado Springs: NavPress, 1988), 32.
4. F. J. Foakes-Jackson, *The Acts of the Apostles, The Moffatt New Testament Commentary* (New York: Harper and Brothers, 1931), xvi.
5. Edgar Blake, "Effective Preaching," *Contemporary Preaching*, ed. G. Bromley Oxnam (New York: Abingdon, 1931), 218.
6. Michael Green, *Evangelism in the Early Church* (Grand Rapids: Eerdmans, 1970), 195.
7. Ibid., 195–96.
8. George Barna, *Never on a Sunday: The Challenge of the Unchurched* (Glendale, Calif.: Barna Research Group, 1990), 24–25.
9. Rick Warren, *The Purpose-Driven Church* (Grand Rapids: Zondervan, 1995), 306.
10. Ibid.
11. Vance Packard, *A Nation of Strangers* (New York: David McKay, 1972), 270.
12. Jean Vanier, *Community and Growth*, rev. ed. (London, England: Darton, Longman & Todd, 1989), 20–21.

CHAPTER SEVEN

FIRING THE RIGHT ARROW

*Preaching is not so much preparing a sermon and
delivering it as it is preparing a preacher and
delivering him.*
—Bishop Quayle

The intent of good biblical messages is not simply to fill up an allotted time slot in the order of worship. The speaker has the more noble purpose of addressing the concerns of the people and hitting the mark in their hearts week in and week out. The content of the message is determined by the needs of the target audience, not by the whimsical desires of the communicator. Homileticians don't mount the pulpit to hear themselves speak, but rather to deliver God's message with power to the listeners. With a correct knowledge of the church consumer, the message doesn't have to be fired with the inaccuracy of a shotgun. Rather, the speaker can aim and fire the truth of God with the pinpoint accuracy of a rifle. Because today's listeners are quick, alert, keen, and discerning—giving the speaker few opportunities to hit the mark—laserlike precision is necessary.

What are the characteristics of a message that hits a moving target with pinpoint accuracy? Putting the following characteristics into practice will help Christian public speakers improve their aim.

CAPTURE THE LISTENERS' ATTENTION

In order to be effective, the message must quickly capture the listeners' attention. The mind of the hearer is on other things, even while at church. The opportunity to score a direct hit will be lost if one fails to promptly shoot the right arrow with laserlike accuracy. This fact places great importance on the introduction of the message. The purpose of the introduction is not to gain the audience's attention, for the speaker already has that. Rather, it is to hook and hold the target audience. In this regard, the first three minutes of the message are crucial. Whether one speaks for twenty minutes or a half-hour, during those initial moments the battle for continued attention is either won or lost.

Ernest Hemingway said that his most anguishing hours as a writer were spent deciding how to begin a novel. After he had developed the plot, the story line, and the main and supporting characters, he would sit with a blank page before him wondering about the way he would grip his readers' attention. Finally, Hemingway would perch in front of the fireplace, carefully peel an orange, and let the skin drop into the fire. As the blue flames sputtered and flickered, the author tried to focus on the one idea that he wanted to communicate. When this became clear, the opening paragraphs of his novel would form in his mind; and he was ready to return to his desk and fill the first blank page, and then hundreds after that.

I can empathize with Hemingway's anxiety over getting started. Staring at an empty page (or a blank computer monitor) can be exasperating. But connecting with one's hearers immediately can add zest and vitality to one's public speaking. I have discovered that I can best capture the attention of the target audience by identifying one of their needs and discussing how it will be met from a biblical perspective. Thus, the introduction establishes the common ground with the listeners by speaking to a concern that is paramount in their minds. When I have taken the preparatory steps outlined in the preceding chapters, I don't have to fret over how I will capture my audience's attention, for I already know.

In flying, the most critical times are the takeoff and the landing. This is also true for public speaking. In order for the message to score a direct hit, I must fire the right arrow, namely, one that touches the needs of the target audience. I can use a well-turned phrase, a compelling illustration, a story about my own struggles, or even a current event to launch and keep the listeners on board.

MEET EXPECTATIONS

The message must meet the expectations of the target audience. The business world places high expectations on people, and upwardly mobile people place high expectations on themselves. Often these same expectations spill over to the church and its leaders and ministries. For instance, the listeners are at church to encounter God. *Why else would they come to the worship service?* If Christianity is true and if it really works, then one would expect to hear a message that is not stilted, stale, or stiff. The hearers expect a sermon that is sincere, stimulating, and spirited.

Because Christ has risen from the dead, His church and the messengers who speak from His pulpit should show evidence of being spiritually alive. This does not mean that the homiletician should substitute energy for unction and sensationalism for truth. Abraham Lincoln once said that he liked to hear people speak publicly as though they were swatting bees. He knew that mere activity can never take the place of effective public speaking. The implication is clear. The target audience wants speakers to show evidence that both they and their message are filled with life.

Public speaking should not be like a funeral dirge. The sin of being boring as a communicator is grievous, indeed. It will not be tolerated by today's audience. When we consider the drama of human redemption and the eternal need of our target group, the messages we deliver will never again be dull or uninspiring. People come to church with the expectation that the message will point them to God. The speaker therefore must never disappoint them.

SPEAK TO PARTICULAR NEEDS

The message must speak to the needs of the target audience. Ninety-one percent of non-Christians believe that the church is insensitive to their needs.[1] And in the eyes of our self-centered, consumer-oriented society, that is the ultimate failure. But once the speaker knows the needs of the listeners, then he or she can establish common ground, capture their attention, address their felt needs, and guide them to the truth of God's Word. Christian public speaking should touch the listeners at the level of their deepest need. And when it does, it allows them to have an encounter with God.

Homileticians present the Word of God to real people with genuine hurts. One noteworthy characteristic of affluent people is that they can cover up their emotional pains. Hidden behind well-manicured lawns, fashionable clothes, and exotic vacations lurk their questions, fears, and hurts. Messages that ignore or neglect these needs will not attract many hearers. When I know that my message is on target, people will later ask me, "Has my spouse been talking to you about me?" or "I felt as if you were speaking directly to me," or "Have you been reading my diary?" or "How did you know that I was struggling in this area?"

PROVIDE A SPIRITUAL BENEFIT

People today live and work in places where cost/benefit analysis is done on a routine basis. And each day consumers analyze the benefits of products, decisions, and personnel. In many respects that inbred way of thinking takes place when they attend church and listen to you speak. The message thus must provide a spiritual benefit to the target audience.

As people listen to you present your message, they're asking, "So what?" Your target audience couldn't care less about the alliterations, movements, and composition of your messages. Rather, they are concerned about bettering themselves. They want to know how the message will help them tomorrow to become loving spouses, effective parents, successful employees, and tender friends. They want you to tell them how the Bible relates to a pluralistic society. They want someone to tell them *how to make a life, not just a living*.

Aren't we all like this? We don't just buy newspapers; we also buy news. We don't simply purchase spectacles; rather, we also want better vision. We don't pay for goopy chemicals called cosmetics. Instead, we shell out big bucks for them to give us beauty and good looks. Millions of drills have been sold. Yet not a single person wanted one. They were actually buying holes. Likewise, people come to you week after week, not to critique your oratory skills, but to benefit from your message. If you can discover what they need and provide it, you will have fired the right arrow at your target audience.

CHALLENGE THE INTELLECT

Your message must challenge the intellect of your listeners, for today's target audience is highly educated. In contrast to previous generations, people today are often better educated than the speaker. A message that does not make sense or is simplistic will disappoint and frustrate your listeners. Sermons today need to challenge people to think, stretch their minds, and answer tough questions.

Theology challenges the mind. While people don't normally think theologically, the speaker's task is to help them do so from a biblical perspective. Pointing out the flip side of a proposition or belief will propel the mental gears of your target audience. Stepping back and helping them understand why certain concepts (such as the fatherhood of God or His creative role) disturbs many in our society will facilitate the thinking of your group. Public speaking needs to stretch people mentally. Stimulating messages communicate hard science, theoretical physics, and other disciplines along with sound theology. This approach will capture and hold today's listeners.

Your access to the minds of your target audience is a terrible opportunity to waste. Therefore, you need to engage their thinking. When you snag their intellect and broaden their understanding, you've wrested their attention for the sake of Christ.

DON'T WASTE THE LISTENERS' TIME

You must ensure that your message doesn't waste the time of your target audience. We live in a busy, fast-paced society. Listeners have little discretionary time. They feel as if they are making a great sacrifice to attend church and give up an hour or two of their day. Thus, your messages must strike a chord with them. And once it is struck, you must play the note that most resonates with them.

As an effective Christian public speaker, you must refuse to bore your listeners with irrelevant information. Instead, get to the core of their life. After all, they're giving you some of their time—the currency of today—and it's best not to shortchange them. You must stir their hearts and send them forth with new power from beyond, new hope for today, and new instruction for dealing with the messy issues in their lives. Your target audience wants to hear what God has to say to them in the midst of their confusions. When they receive His message, they feel as if their time has not been wasted.

ASSIST WITH RAISING THE LISTENERS' FAMILY

Make sure that your messages help the listeners raise their family. In a conversation that I had with a church growth consultant, Lyle Schaller, he asked me, "Do you know what the best slogan is for a church?" "No," I replied, "what is it?" "The best slogan is this: 'We will help you raise your kids!'" "Oh," I said dryly, "that's a good slogan." "No. No," Schaller retorted, "this is not a good slogan; it's the *best* slogan."

Your messages will always hit home when they help your target audience to develop a stronger family, healthier children, and more loving marriages. Of course, not every message you deliver can deal with the family component of life. Nevertheless, a steady diet of public speaking that focuses on parenting, marriage, and family issues is a must.

ACCURATE IN PRESENTING FACTS

When you deliver a message, you must know the facts and present them accurately. With today's sophisticated target audience, you won't be able to wing it anymore. The people in the pew have read the books and newspapers, and they've heard the facts before listening to you present them. Therefore, your message must never insult the listeners' knowledge of world events, statistics, and domestic problems.

Nothing will blow your credibility faster than when you misrepresent your facts or fail to report your information accurately. Specific and precise facts not only give a stronger impact to your message but also quietly convey the notion that you did your homework. Attention to accuracy can serve you well even beyond the immediate message. When you are precise in what you say from the pulpit, you win the right to speak to your target audience again and enjoy their continued trust.

FILLED WITH INTEGRITY

Integrity is something that's hard to get and easy to lose. Thus, when you publicly speak before your target audience, you must be genuine with them. Remember, your listeners are bright and alert. They can tell when you're trying to be someone other than yourself. After all, they live in the real world and can easily detect when someone they know is out of character. Many of them are paid great sums of money to study other people. They can instantly spot a canned message and a freeze-dried messenger. Don't think that you can fool them, for they have listened to plenty of windy "inspirational" talks at conferences, in conventions, and on tape. Thus, it's best for you to be authentic with your constituents. Don't forget that cheap imitations are just that, cheap!

Aristotle believed that character is the most potent of all the means of persuasion. John A. Broadus, the father of American homiletical teaching, said, "Nor must we forget the power of character and life to reinforce speech. What a preacher *is*, goes far to determine the effect of what he *says*. There is a medieval proverb, 'If a man's life be lightning, his words are thunders.'"[2]

The walk of our life must match the words of our messages for there to be integrity. I would be a hypocrite if I challenged my target audience to evangelize the lost and refused to do so myself (by actively building relationships with seekers in order to share Christ with them). I cannot talk about financially supporting the work of the church if I am not a generous giver. It would be foolish for me to offer counsel on effective parenting if I am neglecting my role as a father. Regardless of the topic, the integrity of the message is tied directly to the character of the messenger.

BE RELEVANT

Tragically, many messages begin at eleven o'clock *sharp* on Sunday morning and end at twelve o'clock *dull*. Why? It's because of the irrelevancy of the sermon. The gospel is not just for eternity, but also for today. Your messages need to bring the Bible into the everyday life of your target audience. Your concern is not to make the Bible relevant, for it is already. Rather, you must ensure that your messages are relevant.

Sadly, many who listen to Christian public speakers think that they are woefully out of touch with reality. The unchurched especially think that ministers don't live in the real world and therefore are clueless about what's going on around them.

In order to keep my messages relevant, I try to read at least one weekly news magazine (such as *Time*) and the daily newspaper. I also watch television news programs and listen to all-news radio stations when I'm driving in the car. Doing these things helps me to fire the right arrow at my target audience. I know of one minister who holds a focus group each Thursday before he delivers his message on Sunday. He stays in touch by eating lunch with several people from diverse backgrounds and hearing from their perspectives.

When I first started Christian public speaking, I wrote down the following encouragement from the great Presbyterian preacher and former Chaplain of the United States Senate, Peter Marshall:

> You must root your preaching in reality, remembering that the people before you have problems, doubts, fears,

and anxieties gnawing at their faith. Your problem and mine is to get behind the conventional fronts that sit row upon row in the pews. Consider, for example, the needs of the people who will come to hear you preach. Use your imagination, especially as you try to deal with the problems that are most real to them. If, when you write your sermons, you can see the gleaming knuckles of a clenched fist, the lip that is bitten to keep back tears, the troubled heart that is suffering because it cannot forgive, the spirit that has no joy because it has no hope, if you can see the big tears that run down a mother's face, if you can see these things—then preach them, preach for them—and get down deep.

TRANSLATE THE GOSPEL

Christian public speakers must translate the gospel into today's language. Well-known evangelical theologian Millard Erickson (Distinguished Professor of Theology at Baylor University's Truett Seminary and at Western Seminary, Portland, Oregon) offers a helpful distinction in the use of the terms "translation" and "transformation." He says that every generation must "translate" the gospel into its unique cultural context.[3] This concept is different from "transforming" the message of the gospel into something that was never intended by God in His Word. Those who transform the gospel are improperly trying to turn the good news into something that it is not in order to make it more palatable to their listeners. But those who translate the gospel are keeping the message intact while using different modes to communicate it in ways that connect with their target audience.

The gospel must constantly be translated because the audience keeps changing. Just as the New Testament was written in everyday Greek—the street language of the first century A.D.—so too you must present messages in ways that everyday people can understand. Your target audience doesn't want to hear archaic sermons. Rather, they want you to deliver messages that accurately communicate the meaning of the original text in natural, easy-to-understand English. Your constant challenge will be to present the timeless truths of Scripture to your listeners in ways that are fresh and relevant.

COMMITTED TO EXCELLENCE

You must be committed to excellence in your public speaking. Why? It's because your target audience lives in a polished, professional world. Businesses have made a commitment to excellence. Lee Strobel observed, "While the secular world is pursing excellence in business and industry, many sermons are mired in mediocrity, and that's a major stumbling block in communicating to people."[4]

Excellence in public speaking does not mean being *the* best pulpiteer but rather being *your* best. Quality is not to be measured by the potential of other homeliticians or by their achievements. Instead, it's measured by your own potential. Excellence requires a sense of urgency in which you imagine that you're delivering your last message. Your target audience wants to see in you a passion for them, for life, and for the gospel. They must sense that your words concern eternal matters, not trivial pursuits.

Excellence demands that you proclaim God's truth in ways that match your style of public speaking. Remember, there are different ways to communicate a message. For example, if you are adept at teaching, a more didactic style may emerge. If you are good at encouraging, then your preference may be to speak in a consoling tone. If your focus is pastoral care, your sermons may take on a relational quality. Because you're committed to excellence, you should develop your unique homiletical style and speak from that vantage point.

Excellence necessitates that you devote time to understand the biblical text and your target audience. Quality public speaking also means allowing others to evaluate your sermons on a consistent basis. Don't be afraid to let a few trusted peers thoroughly scrutinize the way you deliver your messages. Their constructive feedback can help you to improve yourself and achieve excellence.

FOSTER RELATIONAL ROOTS

Your messages should foster relational roots, for the people in your target audience may not otherwise stick around long enough to build deep, lasting friendships. In his book *We, the Lonely People,* Ralph Keyes says that above all else Americans value mobility, privacy, and convenience.[5] Those three values make developing a sense of community almost impossible in a church.

Mere church attendance also doesn't help foster a sense of connectedness between people. David Smith characterized the church as "a place where Christians live alone together."[6] All too frequently the congregation is filled with friendly *strangers*. Yet preaching can challenge and foster relational roots. Your messages must encourage the establishment of authentic relationships, real accountability, unconditional forgiveness, and unmitigated compassion. Yes, this is an enormous challenge! But with God's help, it can be done.

DISPLAY A SENSE OF HUMOR

Your messages should contain an element of humor. After all, we live in a serious world that has sapped the joy out of most people. Your sermons can poke holes at the stupidity of our world while prodding your target audience to find answers for their problems from God's Word. You shouldn't be like a clown performing on stage; but you also should not be sour in your public speaking.

Don't always take yourself so seriously. Loosen up, lighten up, and live it up should be the key elements of today's homiletical treatise. Humor allows for the mental equivalent of a seventh-inning stretch in a message. Your target audience needs a mental pause now and then, and humor can supply it in a way that enhances your message.

Critical for your listeners is a sense of coherence between your humorous story and the overall message they're hearing. Thus, when you use humor, make sure that it is relevant to the content of your message. While a motivational speaker or professional humorist can drop in humor that has only a slight connection with the talk, a homiletician cannot. George Sweazy wrote, "Humor in sermons has to stay within the main channel of the thought. If it makes no real contribution in clarifying or applying what the sermon is trying to convey, it has to be left out."[7]

DISPLAY AN AWARENESS OF
THE INFLUENCE OF TELEVISION

Your messages should display an awareness of the influence of television on your target audience. Regardless of how you feel about the matter, this generation has been strongly influenced by the media, especially television. Consequently, your listeners are more prone to be visual than auditory in their style of learning, and your messages should reflect this. For example, try to make your sermons come alive with ideas and stories that are graphic and grabbing, and delivered in a minimal amount of time. Calvin Miller noted that the movement of the message is akin to a billboard. As people drive down the highway, the billboards get only a blink from passing motorists. In light of this, the message should be economical in its use of words, well-crafted in its organization, and narrow in its focus.[8] The presence of these qualities will enable your listeners to trace the theme of your message and remain attentive to its main points.

ENCOURAGE

Your messages should uplift and motivate people to follow Christ. As life unfolds, it is characterized by adversity and triumph, sadness and joy. During any given worship service, the Christian public speaker will encounter numerous hurting people. Because of this, the message should project consolation to the target audience. The words you speak should give them courage in the face of difficulties and hope in the midst of despair. Your sermon should also urge them to remain Christ's obedient followers. The heart of encouraging public speaking is announcing the good news of salvation in Christ.

Hebrews 3:13 instructs us to encourage one another on a daily basis. The Greek verb rendered "encourage" means to stir up, provoke, or incite people in a given direction. The idea is of one person accompanying another on a journey. The companion invigorates the traveler to continue the journey despite obstacles and fatigue. As a Christian public speaker, your job is to uphold your target audience with comforting, lifesaving words.

A good public speaker does not stand "up there" on the platform, far away and concealed from the people. Rather, he or she stands in the midst of the target audience. The compassionate homiletician so encourages the listeners that it pulls them out of their despondency. The speaker affirms the value and significance of the group in the eyes of God. They learn that they are not alone in their hardships, for even the speaker experiences similar struggles in life.

Encouraging public speaking helps the target audience to see the constructive possibilities in every difficult experience. They come to see that life is not wasted when they experience tragedies. For example, initial feelings of doubt and dejection can lead to a stronger faith. Pain and loss can blossom into a more obedient life. One can learn from sin a deeper understanding of God's love and grace. Such comfort, healing, and growth are made possible through faith in Christ.

HAVE A TITLE THAT AROUSES CURIOSITY

Your messages should have titles that arouse the curiosity of the target audience. I heard about a seminary student who took a homiletics course and turned in his first persuasive sermon assignment. His professor returned it with a grade of "D." Concerned and perplexed, the student asked, "Why the low grade?" "The title," said the professor. "You know how to write and deliver a good sermon. But your title is dry and uninteresting." The professor pressed on, "Even your sermon title should be so alluring that when people ride past the church on a bus and see your title on the marquee, they will be irresistibly compelled to come hear you." The student left and returned a day later with the revised manuscript. Proudly, he placed it on the professor's desk. In bold print the new title read, "There's a Bomb on Your Bus."

Developing effective message titles is not easy. The title serves as an attention getter. Through the title we want the target audience to comment before the sermon begins, "Now that's something I want to hear." Since time is a precious commodity to the listeners, they want to know in advance whether the message is going to be beneficial to them. An effective title can assure the group that they will reap dividends from their investment of time.

The title can't be just cute or catchy; it has to touch a genuine need or interest. It should tell the hearers what to expect. The title should also make promises about what is to follow, perhaps in a way that is similar to the title of a *Reader's Digest* article. If the promise is kept by addressing the felt need of the listener with biblical solutions, then he or she will come back week after week.

ENDNOTES

1. George Barna, *The Barna Report,* 1992–1993 (Ventura, Calif.: Regal, 1992), 69.
2. John A. Broadus, cited in Warren Wiersbe, "Advice from the Masters," *Prokope* (Lincoln, Neb.: Back to the Bible, January–February, 1987), 1.
3. Cited in James Emery White, "Analysis: 'Seeker-Targeted' Churches," *Illinois Baptist,* 5 July 1995, 3.
4. Lee Strobel, *Inside the Mind of Unchurched Harry and Mary* (Grand Rapids: Zondervan, 1993), 190.
5. Ralph Keyes, *We the Lonely People,* quoted in David W. Smith, *Men Without Friends* (Nashville: Thomas Nelson, 1990), 169.
6. David W. Smith, *Men Without Friends* (Nashville: Nelson, 1990), 31.
7. George E. Sweazy, *Preaching the Good News* (Englewood Cliffs: Prentice-Hall, 1976), 210.
8. Calvin Miller, *Marketplace Preaching* (Grand Rapids: Baker, 1995), 41–42.

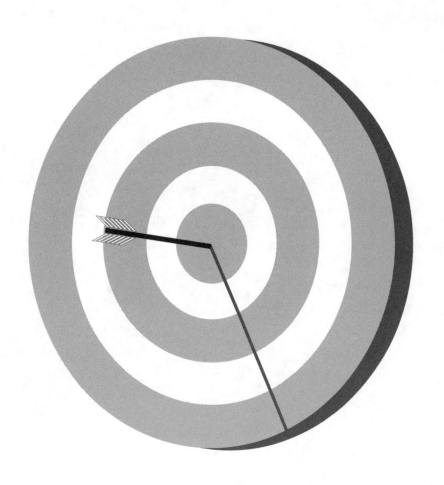

CHAPTER EIGHT

HITTING THE BULL'S-EYE

Some men preach for an hour and it seems like
twenty minutes, and some preach for twenty
minutes and it seems like an hour. I wonder what
the difference is?
—Harry Ironside

You're reading this book because you want to become more effective in your Christian public speaking. In order to do this, you must communicate God's truth by moving from research to marketing to sales. Homileticians, like a successful businessperson, do their homework first by researching the target audience. Then, they develop a message that will address the needs of their listeners. Finally, public speakers endeavor to score a direct hit with their message. In business terms, the orator must "close the sale." This is more difficult than marketing a product, for while the salesperson is trying to change the behavior of people without necessarily changing their beliefs, the speaker is trying to persuade people to change their beliefs as well as their behavior.

Do you remember the old story about the preacher who was talking with a professional baseball pitcher? "I do not understand!" began the pastor. "I am preaching an eternal message, and only a few hundred people show up to hear it. But when you are pitching in a simple game of baseball, an entire stadium is filled to overflowing with thousands of people. What's the difference?" "The difference, I suppose, is in the delivery," replied the baseball pitcher. Whether pitching to hitters or speaking to hearers, one's delivery is crucial to being effective.

The message that hits the bull's-eye moves beyond what one knows *about* the target audience to what one knows *of* the group. It is the ability to see their needs and hurts and show how the power of Christ brings relief. Messages that hit their mark leave an indelible impression on the listeners. Simply speaking, the homileticians that score a direct hit deliver the goods. Like a Cy Young Award winning baseball pitcher, they may not throw the hardest (or speak the loudest), but they possess pinpoint accuracy in their delivery.

THE FUNDAMENTALS

Certain fundamentals enhance the speakers ability to score a direct hit. The fundamentals are posed in the form of questions that need to be asked of every message prior to delivery. Going through this process is essential in gaining knowledge and understanding.

- *What specific need is the message addressing?* No speaker is more effective than the one who knows and relates to a target audience; yet few things are more difficult. It is easy to answer questions that no one is asking and to address needs that are irrelevant. Until I, as a speaker, know the questions and needs of my listeners, the answers that I give are pointless. After engaging in the process outlined in this book, you will have a grasp of the specific needs of your community and target audience. You will also be prepared to relate each message to a specific need, and offer solutions to nagging problems. Remember that Jesus always directed His discourse to the specific needs of His listeners. By employing a similar strategy, you can achieve powerful results.
- *Where is the message going?* The speaker who aims at nothing will hit it every time. However, the target audience will

not appreciate such aimless droning. If someone asks me what my message will be about, I should be able to reply with more than the biblical text of the sermon. If I don't know where my message is going, I may come to the end of the it and find myself all alone. There have been times in my public speaking career when I felt like the pitching prospect who received the following endorsement from a major league baseball scout: "I have good news and bad news. The good news is that he can throw a fastball one hundred miles an hour. The bad news is that no one knows where the ball is going!"

Every message must have a definite aim that can be stated in a simple and direct sentence. For example, I recently spoke on 1 Kings 19—the time when Elijah was running for his life and was physically and emotionally depleted. My one sentence description of the message was, "Help for getting out of the pits." As you can see, stating where the message is going must be definite and precise, and it must be presented clearly early in the message; otherwise, no one will know what you are trying to accomplish. Finding that precise statement is hard work. In fact, it is one of the hardest parts of message preparation. But it is a key to hitting the bull's-eye with your sermon.

- *Why is the message going there?* It's not enough for speakers to declare to the target audience where the message is going. Homileticians must also explain the reason for taking the message in a certain direction. The child in us wants to know the reason why we are called upon to do something. The speaker is wise to keep that in mind as he or she delivers a message.

Behind the stated purpose of the sermon must be a desire to meet the real needs of the target audience. Often the listeners—despite their high level of education—may not understand the reasoning for biblical injunctions. They need to know the scriptural basis for your message, along with the practical benefits of heeding what you say. It is up to you to give these reasons.

For example, in a series on the Ten Commandments, I stated to my target audience that God gave us boundaries and limitations in life. His motive was not to capriciously squelch our enjoyment, but to protect us from harm and provide for our long-term well-being. What appears as negative commands actually contain positive and practical advice. When the listeners understood the reason for the negative commands, it opened their minds and hearts to receive a positive and practical word. Thus, when I help the target audience understand that God's directives are motivated by His great love and concern for their well-being, He becomes someone they want to know intimately.

- *How is the target audience going to get there?* To answer "Where is the message going?" and "Why is the message going there?" without sharing the practical steps of "How is the target audience going to get there?" will lead only to frustration on the part of the listeners. The issue is one of application and the listeners' motivation to take corrective action. The application enjoined by the speaker needs to be as specific as the situation will allow. Or, to say it negatively, the application need not retreat into a level of vagueness that doesn't have any bite. A mentor of mine used to tell me, "Sometimes I am so subtle that no one gets my point!"

When I go to my doctor, I don't want to hear just what is wrong with me. I also want my physician to give me some specific steps on how to get better. People today need fewer "ought-to" sermons and more "how-to" messages, fewer prescriptive sermons and more descriptive messages. "The test of a preacher," according to Francis de Sales, "is that his congregation goes away saying, not 'what a lovely sermon!' but 'I will do something.'"[1] The message should tell the target audience how to behave or believe. A sermon that exhorts the listeners but fails to offer practical instruction is like shouting to a drowning person, "Swim! Swim!" The message may be true, but it isn't helpful.

Any given target audience is generally comprised of 5 percent innovators, 15 percent adapters, and 80 percent adopters. Thus, it stands to reason that most of our hearers will not act on their own. How-to action steps are necessary to help them adopt and apply God's truth. Application can be tested with a three-question quiz.

First, is the application realistic? Can people actually do what is being enjoined? Would I do those things? Sometimes our how-to's are not worth the time and energy. Physically, spiritually, or relationally they are impossibilities. Will Rogers once listened to an admiral describe the menace of German U-boats during the World War I. Rogers eventually raised his hand and asked, "Tell me, can those things operate in boiling water?" "No," the admiral replied, "I'm sure they can't." "Well, then," said Rogers, "you've got your solution. Just boil the ocean." The admiral gave him a blank stare and then muttered, "How?" Rogers sneered, "I gave you the idea. Now you work out the details!"

Second, is the application relational? Is anybody else committed to what is being enjoined? Without a dimension of relational accountability, most applications of God's truth seems to have a built-in fizzle factor.

Third, is the application responsible? Do the admonitions lead people to assume greater culpability for their actions? I don't want to leave any room for my target audience to blame others or count on them unduly for help.

One of the best ways I test the application quotient of my messages is to go over them point by point and ask, "Yes, but how?" In other words, have I told the target audience to do something without showing them how? Clear speaking begins with clear thinking, and clear thinking involves determining what the message is to accomplish in the lives of the listeners. Make sure that the application calls clearly for specific and practical action.

- *Will my listeners' know that I care?* Empathetic communication with the hearers is the proper attitude to convey in
a message. I often hear homileticians remark, "I love to
speak, but I can't stand the audience!" Most likely, the group
can't bear to listen, either. Public speaking that hits the
bull's-eye is done as something you love to someone whom
you love. When a group regards the speaker as someone
who cares for them, they will listen with rapt attention.
After all, they know that the homiletician has their best
interests at heart. And what's more, they rate the speaker
higher than his or her abilities permit.

People often say to public speaking expert Fred
Craddock, "You must come and hear our minister. He's
marvelous." So Craddock goes, and when he hears the
person speak, he concludes that the message should receive a grade of C+. But to the ears of the target audience,
it should be given A+, for the speaker has married them,
buried them, counseled them, and lived among them. In
that context, no one could preach any better!

Effective public speaking identifies with the target audience. Paul is an example of this. He proclaimed, "Jesus
came into the world to save sinners—of whom I am the
worst" (1 Tim. 1:15 NIV). Identification occurs when the
speaker stands before the target audience and announces,
"I know what you experience. I understand the problems
that you face. I recognize the hardships and joys that you
encounter. I've been there, too." The homiletician is no
longer aloof, separated, and uninvolved in the lives of the
listeners, but rather is one of them. Kenneth Burke wrote,
"You persuade a man only insofar as you can talk his language by speech, gesture, tonality, order, image, attitude,
idea, identifying your way with his."[2]

The effective message concludes with a high take-home
value. The speaker takes aim at the response of the target
audience by creating within them a desire to learn more.
The homiletician encourages the listeners to keep living

or thinking in a godly way, to be bold and responsible, or to take action. Because the hearers want something that is usable on the job and at home, the speaker must leave nothing to chance. He or she must clearly state the intended response.

- *What is the scriptural authority for the message?* Effective messages utilize a logical sequence of explanations, stories, vignettes, images, and illustrations that bring the "Why?" and the "How?" of the sermon to life. Yes, it is imperative that these illustrative elements be suitable to real life and relevant to the target audience. Nevertheless, the authority of the message comes from a strong scriptural content. Whether one is speaking from the biblical text or about it, without the support and infrastructure of God's Word, the speaker is giving only his or her opinion.

  A message that is not directly drawn from Scripture is orphaned, regardless of how bright or clever it may sound. *By what authority do you say these things?* is the fervent question of the target audience. A careful study of a biblical text or a series of selected passages where an honest and prayerful engagement occurs gives the speaker a basis for proclaiming divine truth.

- *Will the message make a difference?* The most fatal comment about Christian public speaking is not "It was unbiblical," but rather "That person spoke as though nothing were at stake." Indifference is deadly.

  If we're not careful, we can reduce discipleship merely to being a good person, namely, someone who's good for society. But Christianity demands much more than that. At the end of any message we should ask, "Would Jesus' enemies have executed Him as a result of this?" Not all of my messages stand up to that question. After listening to some of my discourses, the target audience would have been more apt to make Jesus the president of a university or the speaker for a weekend conference. Public speaking becomes invigorated when the message of the church is

presented clearly and forcefully. When the listeners' mind
has been engaged, their heart stirred, their volition altered,
and their spirit reborn, then they know that they have encountered the Savior. The message has hit its mark.

Why do I ask these questions of my messages? It's because
any time I stand to address a target audience, the listeners are
asking, *Why should I pay attention to this person?* Does he care?
Can I trust him? Does he know what he is talking about? Is he
speaking from a higher authority? Unless the target audience can
receive reasonable answers to their questions, my communication with them will be greatly hampered, if not hindered alto-
gether. But if I have done my homework, I have the best
opportunity to communicate dynamically and persuasively. Once
these fundamentals are ingrained in the speaker's preparation,
he or she can consider the content of the message, or the arrows
to be fired at the target audience.

THE CONTENT OF THE MESSAGE

Paula Mergenhagen once wrote, "Life transitions make for
good business opportunities."[3] Life transitions also make for good
public speaking opportunities. Getting married, the birth of a
child, retirement, going off to college, changing jobs, and moving into a new community are all transitional moments that provide a crisis experience where one is more vulnerable and
sensitive to God's Word. But it is the stress, the hunt for fulfillment, the openness to change, the need for relationships, the
open wounds of pulling away from friends and loved ones only
to try to attach to someone new during the relocation of a family that cries the loudest for help in target audiences that are filled
with mobile people.

People experience specific emotions to certain changes in their
lives, and they don't know why. Part of the task of the speaker is
to help people understand why they're experiencing certain
feelings, such as rootlessness, fear, or depression. The speaker
should then offer solutions, care, and answers from a biblical

perspective. When people are in times of transition, they are most open to heed God's Word. The homiletician therefore must not fail to deliver the goods. To enable you to score a direct hit, keep in mind the following about your target audience.

People Resist Establishing Roots

Too often transferred people, especially those who have moved for the first time in their life, are anxious to return home. They make only temporary plans. They fail to empty all their boxes, to change their automobile's license plate, to get a new driver's license, to hang pictures on the wall, or to join a church. They live for tomorrow and dream about returning "home."

These people need to be reminded that life cannot grind to a halt because they are in an unpleasant place. Our messages should encourage hearers to make the best of the situation, to get involved with the community, to enjoy the amenities that a new city has to offer, and to care for the city and the people in the new community.

I have told my target audience about the day lilies that were growing on my lawn. I love day lilies, not just because they are beautiful, but also because they are almost impossible to kill. I have relocated them all over my yard. If I can't get grass to grow somewhere, I just transplant some of those day lilies to that dusty, grassless patch of yard. And when I do, they may not bloom the first season, but give them time to adapt to their new environment, and they will produce the most beautiful flowers!

I remind my target audience that the human organism is a lot like a day lily. When people are relocated and replanted, they tend to remain dormant and feel lost, lonely, and barren. But that is only for a season, especially if they put down roots. When their roots are established in the soil of relationships and routines, then the sprout of life begins to appear, and finally the spirit blooms. The colors unfold, and life is vibrant once again. The secret is to put down the roots and give oneself some time to grow. Oswald Chambers wrote, "Many of us refuse to grow where we are put; consequently, we take root nowhere."[4]

People Fail to Trust in God's Plans

God can do great things in a moving experience. Though people may feel cut off from their family and friends, they are not cut off from God. He does not bring people to a new place to abandon them. Jeremiah 29:11 records perhaps the most beautiful and touching words that God declared to those who had been uprooted from their homeland. "'For I know the plans I have for you,' declares the Lord, 'plans to prosper you and not to harm you, plans to give you hope and a future'" (NIV).

Susan Miller, in her book entitled *After the Boxes Are Unpacked*, describes how she felt when her family moved from the Atlanta, Georgia, area to Raleigh, North Carolina. She left behind her dream house. Though she was excited about her husband's promotion, she didn't want to move. She had found at the end of her rainbow a house that she loved, and it was in Georgia, not in North Carolina.

As the family drove away, all that Susan could see in the rearview mirror was that wonderful, cozy home. It had become her security and her identity. It was the place where she felt that she belonged. But as a result of that move, she wrote what she had learned: "My security does not come from a house. Real security comes from trusting God. I will never grow if I always stay in my comfort zones. Spiritual maturity comes in learning to depend on God to meet my needs. Things should not be held too tightly. They can keep me from embracing what God has planned for me." Yes, Susan Miller had come to trust in God's plan for her life.

Our public speaking needs to communicate that the Lord's plan is an expression of His love for us. Never will the outworking of His purpose fall short of His infinite compassion for us. He always has in mind what is best for us. He'll take any situation that believers are experiencing—even if it is a terrible one—and use it to glorify His name.

When we submit to God's will for us, we will encounter uncertainties, changes, and new ventures. Why? It's because God wants us to live by faith. We need to encourage our listeners to trust in God, not in a company; to find security in God, not in a home; and to depend on God, not on friends and relatives. The Lord's plan is spiritually prosperous and filled with hope. It is one that will result in eternal good for His people. God desires that they trust in the outworking of His will. They can do so, for they know that He has not abandoned them. He nourishes hope, satisfies their deepest eternal longings, and fulfills His promises to them.

People Focus on Themselves

My choice of which graduate school to attend was made on the basis of a girl whom I liked. Yes, other factors were involved, but the main consideration was that I was seriously dating an art student. She was a sophomore when I was a senior in college. She informed me that she would consider transferring to another school as long as it had a top-rated art department. Of my choices of seminaries, Midwestern Seminary in Kansas City was the closest to a top-ranked art school, Kansas University in Lawrence, which was forty miles away.

So I enrolled and headed out to Kansas City with my serious relationship to follow. But she didn't. I found myself in a strange city, and I was furious that my girl friend had reneged on our deal. I was unable to find the kind of friends I had left behind in college, and this made me homesick.

That's when I decided to visit with a favorite professor. I expressed my frustration by saying, "I'm so angry at my girl friend. I'm bitter that I was willing to make such a sacrifice. Now that I'm here, I can't seem to fit in. I wonder whether I have made a mistake. I wonder whether I shouldn't go home." The professor said, "Rick, do you hear what you're saying? Could it be that you have your focus on the wrong person? You have just undergone a major change, a major transition. The feelings that you have are normal. But the important matter during this crisis is to seek God. He has given you a wonderful gift."

"What do you mean?" I asked. "You're in a new place. You have not made a lot of friends. And you're not working. In other words, your distractions are minimal. What a splendid opportunity for you to get to know God better." "I have never thought about it that way before."

This experience from my past has enabled me to comfort my target audience during their times of transition. And I tell them that their move represents a splendid opportunity. After they have unpacked their boxes, hung their pictures on the walls, and placed their tools in the garage, they need to take time to focus on God and deepen their relationship with Him. I remind my target audience that relocating can be a crisis experience. In our English vernacular, we tend to view the word *crisis* in a negative context. Compare our colloquial definition to the Chinese word for *crisis*, which is composed of two picture-characters. One means "danger," whereas the other means "opportunity."

A move presents a crisis in *both* senses of the word. It could be *dangerous* to one's emotional, physical, and spiritual health, especially if one chooses not to rely on God and seek Him. Conversely, a move could be a marvelous *opportunity* to broaden one's horizons, to grow in God's grace, and to experience Him in new and powerful ways. William Morrow wrote, "What lies behind us, and what lies before us, are tiny matters compared to what lies within us." A move offers a tremendous opportunity for us to find our loving and faithful God operating within our life.

People Are Fearful

Fear is a major part of life. It is a God-given emotion. To be afraid is normal. Yet, if fear is out of control, it can be the most paralyzing emotion of all. Fear makes people doubt their abilities and paralyzes the free use of their talents. It brings on "cold feet," makes one a "chicken," and eats away at one's "guts." Fear causes one to miss a sure two-foot putt, a free throw in the closing seconds of a game, a budding opportunity for financial gain, or establishing a friendship that could last a lifetime. Fear motivates one to make more money "just in case of an emergency"; to have the resume always handy, for "you never know when it will be needed"; and to look over one's shoulder, for "you can't trust anyone."

In ancient Greek, the word translated "fear" meant *flight*. It's the picture of pheasants being flushed from their nesting areas and taking flight because they have been alarmed by the approaching danger of a hunter. It's the soldier in battle fleeing the enemy to avoid being shot. "Did you hear those bullets?" asked one soldier to another. "Twice," he said, "once when they went past me and once when I passed them."

While fear is present when we experience transitions in life, it does not have to paralyze us. Moving to a new community, changing jobs, making new friends, and attending a new church can all be fear-producing events. But they don't have to erode our joy and fulfillment in life.

You can hit the bull's-eye in your message by reminding your target audience that an antidote for fear exists. Isaiah wrote, "But now, this is what the Lord says . . . 'Fear not, for I have redeemed you; I have summoned you by name; you are mine'" (Isa. 43:1 NIV). In fact, the command "fear not" appears many times in the Bible. Like a daily vitamin, God has provided just what is needed to help us conquer our fears.

We often need to communicate this antidote for fear. People can face their fears with fact. God says that we do not have to fear, for His presence accompanies us through the unpredictable events of life. He has stated, "When you pass through the waters, I will be with you; and when you pass through the rivers, they will not sweep over you. When you walk through the fire, you will not be burned; the flames will not set you ablaze. For I am the Lord, your God, the Holy One of Israel, your Savior; I give Egypt for your ransom" (vv. 2–3 NIV). God says that we can face any new situation, for He walks with us through the ordeal.

People Refuse to Let Go

When I go to the circus, I'm enthralled by the trapeze artists. Those high-wire performers swing on their trapezes far above the ground under the dome of the circus tent. As they launch out into the void to perform their spins and somersaults, they have to release one trapeze just at the right moment, hover in mid-air for another moment, and then catch hold of the other trapeze. As I watch, I can identify with the anxiety associated with these transitions—the performers letting go of their first support before seizing the second one. Yet it is only by letting go that they can experience the wonder of their feats.

Paul Tournier wrote, "We must always be letting go . . . leaving one place in order to find another, abandoning one support in order to reach the next, turning our backs on the past in order to thrust wholeheartedly toward the future."[5] Letting go of the past is not easy, especially for folks who have unexpected and unwelcome change. As a Christian public speaker, I remind my target audience that when they relocate—letting go one place for another—they do not erase all their past memories of family, friends, and experiences. But in order to make a healthy adjustment to new surroundings and challenges, they need to let go of the past—those habits, fears, controlling influences, and people that are preventing them from taking a step in a new direction. In other words, they need to release the ties and traditions that hold them back from a new opportunity. They need to leave behind any encumbrance that trips them from moving on with their lives.

I did not learn to swim until I was eleven years old. I always had a healthy respect for the water. I was cautious, to say the least. When my wife and I were vacationing in Cancún, Mexico, we decided to go snorkeling. Mostly she decided and I went along. We were taken by boat out to an area that supposedly had beautiful coral reefs and exotic fish. The water was choppy that day, and I spent more time spitting salt water out of my snorkel than looking at fish. A couple of times I was sure that I was drowning. I was ecstatic when I planted my feet on dry land.

A few years later my wife and I spent a week on Maui. While we were there, people said, "You have to go snorkeling!" A favorite place for the locals and vacationers was a short walk down the beach from where we were staying. Again, my wife wanted to go, and again, I complied, even though I harbored painful memories from my Cancún experience. We proceeded to the water, which was peaceful and calm. As we swam out from the shore, we discovered beneath the water's surface the most beautiful rock formations that created a natural aquarium, with the most beautiful fish swimming in all directions. It was truly a sight to behold. The calm water made for a delightful experience. But I experienced it only as I let go of my past fears and reluctance. If I had held onto those past memories, I would never have experienced one of life's serendipitous moments.

Public speaking that hits the moving target often aims at the fear people have of letting go. During times of transition, their fears are heightened. Through your messages, you can encourage them to get guidance and strength from God through His Word.

People Want to Start Over

Don came to our church for a short time. He had moved to our community from another state. He had left behind a broken marriage, a disappointing job, and habits that were inappropriate for a believer. He was on a downward spiral to disaster. "Why did you move here?" I asked. "To start over," he said. "I'm looking for a new beginning."

People on the move need to be reminded that the future is a wonderful place, for it has a redeeming value and quality to it. The future provides an exciting opportunity to begin again or to start over. The Lord is the God of that which is new. For instance, He gives us a new birth, a new life, a new beginning, a new song, a new creation, and a new day. God loves to change a dry, parched, barren, and lifeless soul into a fruitful, fulfilling, and beautiful life.

In the popular movie entitled *City Slickers*, the three main characters are urban dwellers who go to a New Mexico ranch while on vacation to drive a herd of cattle to Colorado. In one scene Phil, whose affair with an employee threatens his marriage, cries to his friends, "My life's a dead end. I'm almost forty years old. I've wasted my life." One of his friends responds, "No. You got a chance to start over. Remember when we were kids playing ball. And the ball would get stuck in the tree. And we would yell, 'Do over!' Your life is a 'do-over.' You got a clean slate." Our messages need to affirm that life offers "do overs." Yes, God loves to give people another chance.

People Need to Move Forward

A new community, a new job, a new school, and a new church may be the doorway to new opportunities and new horizons. But that doorway must be stepped through in order to experience God's blessings. Our messages, therefore, must motivate people to move forward with their life. Oswald Chambers puts it in perspective. "It is no use to pray for the old days; stand square where you are and make the present better than any past has been. Base all on your relationship to God and go forward, and presently you will find that what is emerging is infinitely better than the past ever was."[6]

God has always challenged His people to move forward, and He eternally rewards them for doing so. When the Israelites were leaving Egypt in a mad dash, they came to the Red Sea and were momentarily stopped. What did they do? They panicked and wanted to go back to Egypt, for they feared the unknown. That's when God said to Moses, their leader, "Why are you crying out to Me? Tell the sons of Israel to go forward" (Exod. 14:15 NASB).

Some forty years later, a new generation of Israelites encountered another body of water—the Jordan River. It was not as big as the Red Sea, and no one was pursing the Israelites from the rear. Nevertheless, they were still apprehensive. To Joshua, who was now leading the Israelites into the promised land, God said, "Three days from now you will cross the Jordan here to go in and take possession of the land the Lord your God is giving you for your own" (Josh. 1:11 NIV).

In each scenario God commanded His people to move forward. Faith was required. In fact, it's always required to move forward for God. To meet the challenges of a new day, to move ahead in life, and to grow, trust in the Lord is necessary. It is only as believers move forward in total dependence on God that the unknown becomes known, that the darkness becomes light, and that the night becomes day.

God has some wonderful new beginnings and some exciting new blessings awaiting those who move forward in faith. Patrick Overton describes the movement and God's corresponding response: "When you walk to the edge of all the light you have and take that step into the darkness of the unknown, you must believe that one of two things will happen. Either there will be something solid for you to stand on, or God will teach you how to fly."

Our public speaking must be rooted and grounded in faith, especially when we proclaim an active and vibrant trust in God. Our faith makes a difference when our life seems uncertain, when we face the unknown, when we make a career change, and when we relocate to a new city. When people are uprooted, they often feel as if the rug of their life has been pulled out from under them. Our messages should instill hope in listeners who are feeling overwhelmed by unanticipated changes. They need to know that God will catch, support, and encourage them, thus softening the blow of the fall. He can be trusted.

People Are in the Pit of Despair

People who have been relocated often feel like the cartoon character Joe Btsfplk in the Li'l Abner comic strip. Al Capp always drew a black rain cloud hanging just over Joe's head. This is a great picture of depression. It depicts someone feeling gloomy and lonely. People who have been forced to relocate feel the walls of life crashing in them and the dark cloud of depression hovering over them. While others are romping in the sunshine of joy, they are in the pit of despair.

But God has a better idea. He doesn't want anyone to stay in the pits, and He doesn't want anyone to wallow in self-pity. He does not give up on people who are feeling bitter and lonely. The Lord wants to say something to them and do something for them. God can use our public speaking to make known His truth and will. Effective oratory can help a target audience to redirect their focus from themselves to God. Rather than allow the hurt of relocating to become a wedge between them and God, it can be a catalyst to draw them near to Him.

People Need to Hear the Truth of God

God is like a rescuer for someone lost and trapped in a cave. As long as the person is fearful and screaming, he or she will not hear the sounds of the rescue party. Similarly, panicky people can't hear God amid the noise and restlessness of their life. The Lord can be heard, but only if one will listen.

A farmer from the Midwest was visiting his college roommate in New York City. While the farmer was walking near Times Square one day, he suddenly remarked, "I hear a cricket." "You're crazy!" his city friend quipped. "It's the noon rush hour, and in all this traffic noise you heard a cricket? C'mon, man!" "No, I did hear a cricket," the visitor insisted. Focusing more intently, he walked to the corner, crossed the busy avenue, and looked all around. Finally he approached a shrub in a large cement planter. Digging beneath the cover mulch, he found the cricket.

The visitor's friend couldn't believe what he had seen. But the farmer said, "My ears are no different from yours. It simply depends on what you have learned to hear. Let me show you." He then reached into his pants pocket, pulled out a handful of change, and dropped the coins on the sidewalk. At the sound of the money hitting the pavement, every head along the crowded block turned to look. "You see what I mean?" the visitor said, as he began picking up what was left of his coins. "It all depends on what you are used to hearing."

People on the move have trouble listening to God. They want to hear a word of affirmation from a heavenly voice about whether to make such a move. They are looking for God to answer to their questions as though He would write His message across the sky. The public speaker can remind the target audience that contrary to the way people act, God seldom shouts, rants, or raves. Rather, He quietly leads. From deep inside our soul, we can sense the guidance of God. And oftentimes He uses a message from His Word to give people the courage to face their hardships.

People Are Lonely

Thomas Wolfe, an American novelist, wrote that "loneliness, far from being a rare and curious phenomenon, peculiar to myself and a few other solitary men, is the central and inevitable fact of human existence." Psychiatrists have estimated that between 70 to 90 percent of Americans are chronically lonely. According to Paul Tournier, it is the most devastating problem of this age. Many of us experience loneliness. Transitions (such as a new job, changing schools, retiring, or relocating) only intensify and ignite it.

Humans are largely social beings and therefore must relate to somebody. Dr. Robert S. Weiss of Harvard Medical School insists that loneliness is a perfectly normal response to the lack of two primary social needs. The first is a sense of attachment, provided by an intimate relationship with a spouse or loved one. The second is a sense of community, provided by a network of friends who share similar interests and concerns. The absence of either of these primary relationships (which people on the move experience) results in loneliness.[7] Loneliness, like a magnet, can be the force that drives people together or apart. People in transition should regard loneliness as a gift that spurs them to be in a relationship with God and with others.

One of my first moves resulted in my being transplanted six hundred miles from family. I didn't know anyone in the town where I now lived. People in my new surroundings seemed distant and unfriendly. I was miserable. One day I heard a man remark, "We can make a heaven or a hell where we are; it's just up to us." I started to think about all my old friends many miles away, and I realized that those friendships were not developed over night. In some instances, they took years to form. So I decided to make a heaven out of my new locale. I joined the church I had been attending, and quickly found a place of service. Then I joined a tennis club—both to get into better shape and meet some people. Before long I had a full social calendar.

When I stand before my target audience, I remember how alone I felt being separated from family and friends. But I also remember that my loneliness became the catalyst that moved me toward other people as well as closer to God. As a Christian public speaker, I can be the Lord's megaphone to remind people that loneliness is His way of getting them to move closer to Him in a loving relationship.

ENDNOTES

1. Francis de Sales, cited in "The Pulpit's Personal Side," *Leadership* (spring 1990), 25.
2. Kenneth Burke, cited in Raymond Bailey, "Building an Effective Message," *Preaching* (September–October 1998), 5.
3. Paula Mergenhagen, *Targeting Transitions* (Ithaca, N.Y.: American Demographics, 1995), 237.
4. Oswald Chambers, cited in Susan Miller, *After the Boxes Are Unpacked* (Colorado Springs: Focus on the Family, 1995), 71.
5. Paul Tournier, *A Place for You* (New York: Harper & Row, 1968), 164.
6. Oswald Chambers, cited in Warren Wiersbe, *With the Word* (Nashville: Oliver-Nelson, 1991), 362.
7. Robert S. Weiss, cited in *How to Overcome Loneliness* (New York: Guideposts Associates, 1981), 7.

CHAPTER NINE

TAKING STOCK: DID THE TARGET AUDIENCE GET THE POINT?

Preaching is thirty minutes to raise the dead.
—John Ruskin

A fellow attended a special evening service at the church but sat near the door. After the speaker had droned on for some forty minutes, the visitor got up and left. On the way out, he met a friend coming in. The man asked, "Am I late? What's he talking about?" The fellow replied, "Don't know. He ain't said yet!"

Calvin Coolidge, who never wasted words, came home from church and was asked by his wife, "What did the minister preach about?" "Sin," replied the President in his usual laconic fashion. "Well what did he say about it?" "He was against it." At least Coolidge *knew* what his pastor had said. Not everyone who attends church can recall much about the message.

Vagueness in public speaking, like vagueness in giving directions to a lost person, is an unpardonable sin. As Ruskin has said, a speaker has "thirty minutes to raise the dead." That miracle will never occur if the message is unclear. In every speaking situation, what matters most is this: Did the target audience get the speaker's point? Was the message communicated clearly, forcefully, and convincingly?

At the heart of this book is the fact that people matter to God. He cares about their needs, their questions, and their concerns. To hit a moving target one must know the relevant needs of the audience and address those needs so that the listeners get the undisputed message with clarity. Yes, this task is not easy, for it requires concentration, timing, and pinpoint accuracy. But because people matter to God and to us, we will communicate with them so that they get the point.

Effective communication requires speaking in a way that will encourage people to listen. Public proclamation, as is any form of communication, is a two-way street. If the target audience did not receive the message, the conveyance of information has been incomplete. A quarterback can throw a perfectly spiraled pass toward a speedy receiver downfield. He may hit his moving target in the hands; but if that receiver does not catch the ball, the pass falls incomplete, regardless of how tight the spiral and the beauty of the pass. One fundamental need of great public speaking is an attentive group. I may deliver a well-crafted discourse; but if it is not heard, then the message, like the football pass, falls incomplete.

I have discovered that when I know my target audience better than they know themselves, and when I have addressed the issues and concerns of their lives, my message has a better possibility of scoring a direct hit. My words, while not eloquent or grandiose, gain a hearing because I am speaking in the language of the people. It is similar to when someone is talking about money—that subject always gets the attention of people. But when someone starts talking about *your* money, then you are even more prone to inch closer to the speaker. You're also more likely to bring all your mental faculties to bear on the discussion. That's the same sort of dynamic we seek to achieve from the pulpit.

THE FILM ROOM

How does a public speaker determine whether the target audience has heard the message? How does he or she know whether the sermon has scored a direct hit? A football team has a film room to replay the game and evaluate the effectiveness of each player. In many instances, the coaches will grade the players on their performance after watching the film of the game. Likewise, the speaker needs a group of people who will assist him or her in determining whether the message hit the mark.

Some speakers gather a group of critics to "watch the film," namely, a video of the previous Sunday's message, and offer feedback and helpful comments. Other speakers distribute cassette tapes of the message and ask the critics to comment, either in a group setting or through written evaluation. I know of some homileticians who distribute listening guides to selected worship attenders in order for them to evaluate the message. Ministers at multiple staff churches might evaluate each speaker's message.

Regardless of how the evaluation occurs, a speaker needs a better way to evaluate the effectiveness of the message other than an "exit poll" from comments made by parishioners leaving the worship service, or other than asking one's spouse on the way home from church, "How did I do?" or "What did you think of today's message?"

A formalized system of evaluation is imperative. The development and implementation of that system will vary with each public speaker. But once it is in place, the general feedback that you want to get is simple:

- Was the point of the message communicated?
- Was the message clear?
- What from this message do you remember?
- Was there anything in the message that was foggy?
- What did the message lack?
- How did you feel when you left the church?
- What made you personally involved?

When you recruit your film room critics, make sure that they are discerning and godly people who will lovingly, but truthfully, evaluate each message in written form. Their goal should be to stimulate your public speaking gift so that it will grow and develop. Be sure to ask your critics to begin their comments with encouraging observations. Then have them frame their constructive feedback in the form of recommendations. For example, it's easy for someone to say, "I didn't like point two." But the speaker needs to know, "How would you have changed point two so that it could be better?"

As you formulate a systematic plan to evaluate your messages, keep in mind three important rules. First, avoid a quick-fix mentality or a "finding out what works and then doing it" approach. Improvement comes gradually. It requires you to devote much of your thought and energy to correct specific problems. Second, remember that you are discovering yourself when you learn about your public speaking. You will find out what you naturally do well. Conversely, you will learn what you need to improve. Third, remember that you are communicating biblical truth to the glory of God.

THE GAME PLAN

The challenge of public speaking to a mobile target audience is to score a direct hit consistently. The process outlined in this book takes considerable time, especially in gathering and documenting background information. Yet, the data are invaluable, for they identify and profile the present needs of your community and listeners. You can also use the information you obtain to ensure that your upcoming messages meet the felt needs of your listeners.

Once you have gathered the information that you need, you can plot a yearly public speaking plan that will address the specific concerns of your target audience. Since my church tradition does not use a lectionary, I must personally determine the weekly topics and Scripture texts. In the absence of relevant data, much of my time in study could be wasted in making procedural decisions. By understanding the needs and profile of my target audience, I am better able to determine a public speaking plan for the year. In turn, this process has saved me a great deal of time, energy, and concern.

I begin to design my public speaking plan by using the bands of a target to represent a particular audience. First, there is the culture to consider. What are the issues that are confronting society at large that I should address in my messages? Sermons targeted toward gambling, abortion, and other societal ills would fall into this category. During election years, I develop messages that address character and leadership. The ethics and morality of society, the recent violence in our nation's schools, and the approaching millennium are a few of the many issues that I try to address from a Christian perspective.

Second, I select messages that I can direct toward the community at large. What are the issues that arise from the demographic and psychographic study of my community? I need to regularly address these matters. My community has experienced considerable population growth in recent years that present certain problems for its residents, which go beyond traffic congestion, school overcrowding, and poor service industry. The population increase indicates a lack of community, a need for friends, and a desire for help and encouragement from others. There is also loneliness, depression, and a competition to keep up with one's neighbors and work associates.

The psychographic reporting indicates values, attitudes, and lifestyle issues that I need to address. My community tends to be materialistic and carry a high degree of debt, they are overworked and overcommitted, they have little discretionary time, they struggle to spend quality time with their family, and they are fearful of the future. It is a relatively straightforward process for me to match biblical texts to specific problems or issues in my community. For instance, I know that messages on money management, fiscal responsibility, stress relief, and family problems will capture the attention of my target audience.

Third, an examination of my congregation will indicate the specific needs and concrete issues that I should address each year in my public speaking plan. For example, if the evangelistic fires are damp, messages to motivate and encourage the witnessing zeal of the church are in order. Some of the church's issues are perpetual and addressed on an annual basis, such as a stewardship emphasis or a commitment to ministry and service. In addition, from time to time every congregation needs to be encouraged in what it is doing right. A thorough study of a church will disclose those areas of giftedness and contribution that I can highlight in my messages.

Fourth, I need to consider the specific needs of the consumer. With this knowledge, I design messages and homiletic series that address their particular concerns. In recent years I have presented a series of messages entitled "Living the Good Life." I used the Book of Ecclesiastes to talk about pleasure, religion, money, and time. In a series entitled "Facing Our Fears," I dealt with the apprehension of being alone, facing death, and putting up with a meaningless life. In a series entitled "Power to Overcome," I offered biblical guidelines for overcoming pride, envy, anger, laziness, greed, lust, and gluttony. In a series based on Psalm 23, I gave my target audience biblical counsel for overcoming worry, hurriedness, damaged emotions, indecision, adversity, and hurt.

Whenever I plan a year's worth of public speaking, I try to balance Old and New Testament texts. Approximately half of my messages are expositional, while the other half are topical. I intersperse doctrinal messages and need-related sermons into the public speaking plan in order to maintain a balance.

A COMPLETION

Every public speaker wants to connect with his or her target audience. As I have undertaken the steps outlined in this book, I have become more sensitive to the needs of my listeners. I feel a greater degree of confidence in presenting messages that are focused on their known and stated concerns. A connection exists that enables me to address issues that are prevalent on the minds of the majority of the people in my target audience.

A HERO

I want my public speaking to be personal. Because I know precisely the needs of my target audience, I am able to speak as a friend or witness rather than as an orator. A witness is more effective than a rhetorician. He who cries "fire" in a burning theater need not be an orator. The bearer rates his effectiveness on how fast the theater is cleared, not on the ovation of the customers. The alarmist is not out for encores but empty seats.

The task of my public speaking is personally to rescue hurting, wounded, and drowning people from the agony and pain of their needs by leading them to safety through my messages. I can best accomplish this through a personal witness. I have discovered that public speaking that is personal—namely, from the heart of the speaker to the heart of the listener—will never lack an enthusiastic target audience. When I drop my mask and show my own struggles and weaknesses, the listeners are softened. This allows my sermons to penetrate their hearts and score a direct hit.

IN THE GROOVE

As I put into practice the steps outlined in this book, my public speaking has experienced a new surge of confidence. Because I have done the research and know my people so well, I do not worry about *not* hitting the target. I know that my messages will land on the mark, even though the target is moving. I feel like a baseball pitcher in a "groove" or a basketball player in a "zone." I know that I cannot miss, for my messages will always address a foremost need in my target audience.

As I speak publicly, I find that I communicate friend-to-friend rather than speaker-to-audience. This feeling is hard to describe, but it is definitely present. I understand the pains and hurts of my listeners in a new light. Incidentally, I have come to love them more deeply as a result of employing the steps I have outlined in this book. This process has caused me to draw more intimately on the grace and love of God. Oswald J. Smith was right when he wrote, "The world does not need sermons; it needs a message. You can go to seminary and learn how to preach sermons, but you will have to go to God to get messages."[1]

Christian public speaking is not a task to be envied, for it requires unending toil and preparation. People have varied and

heavy expectations of the speaker. Even to come close to the target week in and week out requires a deep and loving dependence
on God. Without His help, direction, and support, the task becomes a boring and monotonous routine. Because of God's un-
failing grace, new life is breathed into me and courage is fortified
in my soul, especially as I try to hit the moving target of my audience every time I deliver a message.

ENDNOTE

1. Oswald J. Smith, cited in *Leadership* (summer 1987), 19.

APPENDIX

CULTURE—TARGET ASSUMPTIONS
Penetrating Your Culture

1. What do I observe about my world?

2. What do I overhear people saying about my world?

3. What are people saying to me directly about my world?

4. What are my readings indicating to me about my world?

5. What assessment about the present can I make concerning the future?

6. What is God doing in my world?

COMMUNITY—TARGET AREA
Areas of Investigation

1. **Geographic Area:** What is unique and distinguishing about your community?

2. **Demographic Area:**
   - *Population:* What is the population of the community your church serves?
   - *Age:* How many people are in each age group?
   - *Race:* What are the predominant races?
   - *Households:* What are the predominant types of households—family or nonfamily?
   - *Housing:* Do people own or rent their residences?
   - *Household Income:* What is both the mean and the average household income?
   - *Educational Attainment:* What is the educational level of the community?
   - *Mobility:* What is the average length of stay of a resident?
   - *Transportation and Travel to Work:* How long does it take to get to work each day?
   - *Employment:* What types of occupations are predominant?

3. **Psychographic Area:** What do people value and think is important?

4. **Pneumagraphic Area:** What is the spiritual climate of your community?

COMMUNITY—TARGET AREA
Community Profile

1. What do people read?

2. Are the people ambitious?

3. What do the people think?

4. How educated are the people?

5. Are the people happy?

6. What kind of music do the people enjoy?

7. What are the professions of the people?

8. How do the people use their time?

9. How do the people get their exercise?

10. How are the people involved in service or community groups?

11. How do the people feel about themselves?

12. How do the people feel about their families?

13. How do the people feel about religion?

14. How do the people spend their money?

15. How do the people value money?

16. What causes the people stress and fatigue?

17. How do the people play?

18. How do the people work?

CHURCH—TARGET AUDIENCE
Needs Questionnaire

Have the adult segment of your target audience complete the survey at the beginning of the Bible study hour or small-group meeting. However, it can be completed at any time (for example, during specific meetings, before the worship hour, or after receiving the survey in the mail). The best results will come when the respondents are given fifteen minutes to complete the survey and asked to return it immediately. If the survey is given during a program event (such as a Bible study, worship service, or small-group time), have the leader say the following:

> The leadership of our church is interested in ministering to us and our needs more effectively. In order to do this, they must have our input. That's why they have asked us to complete the questionnaire you have in your hands. Everyone should have a survey. Is there anyone who didn't get one? Our responses will be scored and the results will be reviewed by our church leadership. Your responses to the survey will remain confidential. No one will know what you marked on your survey. Please indicate how often the numbered statements on the survey are true of you: "Always," "Often," "Sometimes," "Seldom," or "Never." Please fill in only one answer per statement. If you change your answer, be sure that you completely erase your first mark. We will take the next fifteen minutes to complete this survey before we move on to the rest of our meeting.

CHURCH MEMBERSHIP QUESTIONNAIRE

Your responses to this survey will remain confidential. No one will know what you have marked. This information will be used to assist our pastor and church leadership in meeting the needs of this congregation. Thank you for your cooperation.

PART A—MEMBERSHIP PROFILE

1. **Gender:**
   ___ 1) Male   ___ 2) Female

2. **Age:**
   ___ 1) 18–22
   ___ 2) 23–29
   ___ 3) 30–44
   ___ 4) 45–64
   ___ 5) 65 and above

3. **Race:**
   ___ White ___ Black ___ Asian ___ Other

4. **Marital Status:**
   ___ 1) Single
   ___ 2) Married
   ___ 3) Separated
   ___ 4) Widowed
   ___ 5) Divorced

5. **Housing:**
   ___ Buying ___ Renting ___ Other

6. **Education:**
   ___ High School ___ College ___ Graduate School

7. **How long has your family lived at your present address?**
   ___ 1) Less that five years ___ 2) More than five years

8. **Transportation to Work:**

   Average travel time to work _____

9. **Employment:**

   Identify your occupation _____

PART B—SURVEY OF PERSONAL NEEDS

Tell how frequently these statements are true of you. Please mark the line with an *A* for "Always," *B* for "Often," *C* for "Sometimes," *D* for "Seldom," and *E* for "Never," or *N/A* for "Not Applicable." Please indicate only one answer per statement.

___ 1) I have feelings of insecurity.

___ 2) I worry about debt.

___ 3) I have a satisfying marriage.

___ 4) I think about the future.

___ 5) I feel as if my family has no roots.

___ 6) I feel that I don't understand the Bible.

___ 7) I welcome new friendships.

___ 8) I wonder whether my children will experience a quality of life similar to the one I have.

___ 9) I welcome change.

___ 10) I feel the pressure of many time constraints.

___ 11) I have plenty of friends.

___ 12) I think about making more money.

___ 13) My family lives with unresolved conflict.

___ 14) I wonder where I will live when I retire.

___ 15) I place high expectations on people.

___ 16) God does not seem to be there for me when things are going bad.

___ 17) I feel as if I don't know many people.

___ 18) My inconsistency in raising my children frustrates me.

___ 19) Change is difficult for me to handle.

___ 20) I can't be as committed to outside job pursuits as I would like.

___ 21) I wonder whether I will have enough money to be able to retire comfortably.

___ 22) I would change jobs to receive a higher salary.

___ 23) My loved ones and I have difficulty communicating easily and openly.

___ 24) I think about going "home."

___ 25) I feel lonely.

___ 26) I seek God's direction in making major changes in my life.

___ 27) I feel as if I don't have anyone to talk with about my struggles.

___ 28) My children adjust well to new environments.

___ 29) I wish life were more stable.

___ 30) I welcome a new job assignment so that I can spend more time with my family.

___ 31) I would relocate my family for a higher-paying job.

___ 32) I don't have a sense of purpose.

___ 33) I want to know the benefits of new church programs.

___ 34) I wish I knew God's will for my life.

___ 35) I open up easily to new people.

___ 36) Relocating is harmful to my family's well being.

___ 37) I become restless after living in one place for a while.

___ 38) I feel the stress of overcommitment.

___ 39) My present job has an uncertain future.

___ 40) I worry about my aging parents.

___ 41) I feel used by my employer.

___ 42) I wonder whether God cares where I work or live.

___ 43) I place my family over my career.

___ 44) I have difficulty maintaining relationships.

___ 45) The Bible doesn't seem to offer solutions to the problems in my life.

CHURCH—TARGET AUDIENCE
Church Profile

1. What do the people read?

2. Are the people ambitious?

3. What do the people think?

4. How educated are the people?

5. Are the people happy?

6. To what kind of music do the people listen?

7. What are the professions of the people?

8. How do the people use their time?

9. How do the people get their exercise?

10. How are the people involved in service or community groups?

11. How do the people feel about themselves?

12. How do the people feel about their family?

13. How do the people feel about religion?

14. How do the people spend their money?

15. How do the people value money?

16. What causes the people stress and fatigue?

17. How do the people play?

18. How do the people work?

CHARACTERISTICS OF THE MESSAGE
Questions to Ask for Accuracy

1. Does the message capture the listeners' attention?

2. Does the message meet the listeners' expectations?

3. Does the message speak to the listeners' needs?

4. Does the message provide a benefit?

5. Does the message challenge the intellect?

6. Does the message waste the listeners' time?

7. Does the message assist with raising the listeners' family?

8. Does the message present facts accurately?

9. Is the message filled with integrity?

10. Is the message relevant?

11. Does the message translate the gospel into today's language?

12. Is the message committed to excellence?

13. Does the message encourage relational roots?

14. Does the message display a sense of humor?

15. Does the message reflect an awareness of the influence of television?

16. Does the message encourage and motivate?

17. Does the message have a title that arouses curiosity?

CHARACTERISTICS OF THE MESSAGE
Fundamentals of the Message

1. **Need Basis:** What specific need is the message addressing?

2. **Aim:** Where is the message going?

3. **Purpose:** Why is the message going there?

4. **Application:** How are people going to get there?

5. **Ethical Appeal:** Will my listeners know that I care?

6. **Biblical Basis:** What is the scriptural authority for the message?

7. **Cost of the Gospel:** Will the message make a difference?

CHARACTERISTICS OF THE MESSAGE
Evaluation Form

Date: _____

Message Title: _____

Biblical Text: _____

1. Was the point of the message communicated?

2. Was the message clear?

3. What from this message do you remember?

4. Was there anything in the message that was foggy?

5. What did the message lack?

6. How did you feel when you left the assembly?

7. What made you personally involved?

8. What real or felt need did the message address?

Encouraging words related to the message:

Recommendations for improvement:

DESIGNING A YEARLY PUBLIC SPEAKING PLAN

1. **Culture:** What are the issues confronting society?

2. **Community:** What are the issues facing the local community?

3. **Church:** What are the specific needs confronting your church?

4. **Consumer:** What are the specific needs of individual members?

More Great Resources for Pastors from Kregel Publications, Your Partner in Ministry

Ministry Nuts and Bolts
What They Don't Teach Pastors in Seminary
by Aubrey Malphurs

Pastoral leadership includes more than preaching and teaching. Veteran seminary professor and church planter Aubrey Malphurs explains crucial areas often overlooked: developing unified values, mission, vision, and strategy in your ministry.

ISBN 3190-5   192 pp.

Also available from Aubrey Malphurs:
• *Developing a Dynamic Mission for Your Ministry*
• *Biblical Manhood and Womanhood*
• *Strategy 2000*

Ethical Dilemmas in Church Leadership
Case Studies in Biblical Decision Making
by Michael R. Milco

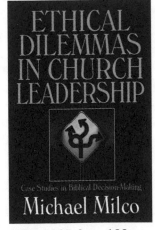

Veteran pastor Michael Milco presents case studies on AIDS, infidelity, child abuse, and more, equiping leaders with the tools to handle sensitive issues and crisis situations that can occur in any church.

ISBN 3197-2   192 pp.

The Christian Message for Contemporary Life
The Gospel's Power to Change Lives
by Stephen F. Olford

Well-known speaker and author Stephen Olford uses 1 Corinthians 1:9–3:4 to examine the life-changing power of the Christian message as seen in Paul's writings.

ISBN 3361-4   128 pp.

Ministry on the Cutting Edge
Maintaining Pastoral Effectiveness and Personal Authenticity
by Rick Ezell

Every pastor has been through times of dullness in spirit and ineffectiveness in ministry. Success in ministry does not depend on marketing and management but on the character, passion, and authenticity of the pastor himself. This book is an encouraging guide for sharpening one's ministry skills for a long-lasting and truly effective life in ministry.

Also available from Rick Ezell:
• *Hitting a Moving Target*

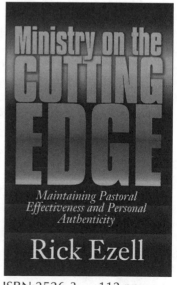

ISBN 2526-3   112 pp.

Pastor to Pastor
Tackling the Problems of Ministry
by Erwin Lutzer

Veteran pastor Erwin Lutzer of the historic Moody Memorial church in Chicago offers encouragement and practical advice on how to handle issues such as church splits, burnout, worship, congregational expectations, and pastoral priorities.

Also available from Erwin Lutzer:
• **The Doctrines That Divide**

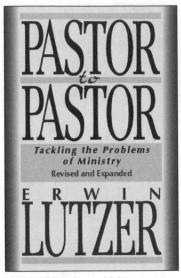

ISBN 3164-6   128 pp.

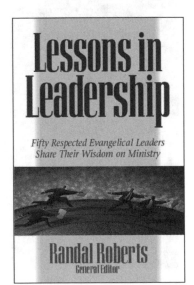

ISBN 3630-3   282 pp.

Lessons in Leadership
Fifty Respected Evangelical Leaders Share Their Wisdom on Ministry
edited by Randal Roberts

Whether you are currently training for ministry, have recently entered into a leadership role, or are looking for fresh insights, you will greatly benefit from the insightful counsel of pastors and ministry leaders such as Bill Bright, Stuart Briscoe, and Carl F. H. Henry.